Multimodal Methods in Anthropology

Multimodal Methods in Anthropology develops several goals simultaneously. First, it is an introduction to the ways that multimodality might work for students and practitioners of anthropology, using multiple examples from the authors' research and from the field. Second, the book carefully examines the ethics of a multimodal project, including the ways in which multimodality challenges and reproduces "digital divides." Finally, the book is a theoretical introduction that repositions the history of anthropology along axes of multimodality and reframes many of the essential questions in anthropology alongside collaboration and access. Each chapter introduces new methods and techniques, frames the ethical considerations, and contextualizes the method in the work of other anthropologists. *Multimodal Methods in Anthropology* takes both students and practitioners through historical and contemporary sites of multimodality and introduces the methodological and theoretical challenges of multimodal anthropology in a digital world. Like multimodality itself, readers will come away with new ideas and new perspectives on established ideas, together with the tools to make them part of their practice. It is an ideal text for a variety of methods-based courses in anthropology and qualitative research at both the undergraduate and the graduate level.

Samuel Gerald Collins is Professor of Anthropology at Towson University in Towson, USA.

Matthew S. Durington is Professor of Anthropology at Towson University in Towson, USA.

Multimodal Methods in Anthropology

Samuel Gerald Collins and Matthew S. Durington

NEW YORK AND LONDON

Designed cover image: Zig Zag Apples, by Georgina Durington

First published 2024
by Routledge
605 Third Avenue, New York, NY 10158

and by Routledge
4 Park Square, Milton Park, Abingdon, Oxon OX14 4RN

Routledge is an imprint of the Taylor & Francis Group, an informa business

© 2024 Samuel Gerald Collins and Matthew S. Durington

The right of Samuel Gerald Collins and Matthew S. Durington to be identified as authors of this work has been asserted in accordance with sections 77 and 78 of the Copyright, Designs and Patents Act 1988.

All rights reserved. No part of this book may be reprinted or reproduced or utilised in any form or by any electronic, mechanical, or other means, now known or hereafter invented, including photocopying and recording, or in any information storage or retrieval system, without permission in writing from the publishers.

Trademark notice: Product or corporate names may be trademarks or registered trademarks, and are used only for identification and explanation without intent to infringe.

ISBN: 978-1-032-36225-0 (hbk)
ISBN: 978-1-032-36224-3 (pbk)
ISBN: 978-1-003-33085-1 (ebk)

DOI: 10.4324/9781003330851

Typeset in Sabon
by Taylor & Francis Books

Contents

	Acknowledgments	*vi*
	Introduction	1
1	Multimodality	10
2	Old Questions and New Directions	38
3	Photography	56
4	Mapping the Community	78
5	Games	93
6	Apps	110
7	Design	125
8	Conclusion	145
	Postscript: The Elephant in the Room	154
	Index	*162*

Acknowledgments

This volume is the result of nearly 20 years of community collaborations, collaborations that precede our theorizations of multimodality by at least a decade. During that time, there have been many, many people and organizations who have been part of our work, each of whom has been instrumental in the development of this book. Although these are too numerous to enumerate in their entirety, special acknowledgment must be extended to: Betty Bland-Thomas, Wide Angle Youth Media, Liberty Grace, Temple X, Greenmount West Community Center, Red Emma's Bookstore, Morgan State University, Coppin State University, the American Anthropological Association and the Society for Visual Anthropology.

In addition, there have been so many students. We're teachers, and our ideas are closely linked to our classes. Over the course of many semesters, we've developed this material in "Visual Anthropology," "Ethnographic Methods," "The Anthropology of Media" and "Design Anthropology." These courses have allowed us to utilize multimodal methods in instruction, and we owe gratitude to our students who have been a sounding board for tweaking methodologies and an emergent pedagogy.

Finally, we want to thank our colleagues. Harjant Gill was the third associate editor in our tenure as multimodal editors at the *American Anthropologist*, and he has been pivotal in developing our ideas. Niki Fabricant has also engaged with multimodality over her exceptional career, and her unwavering commitment to community has sharpened our focus on collaboration in multimodality. David Goldstein and Brigid Hogan at the National Park Service have been wonderfully receptive to our multimodal plans for different NPS projects. Monica Pelayo has grounded us in public history. Krista Harper, Anastasia Salter, and Nick Mizer have been formative in our theorizing on games – and were driving forces behind the establishment of the "AnthropologyCon" workshops where many of our multimodal methodology ideas germinated.

Introduction

As in so much of our collective lives, the pandemic has framed the issues raised in this book. In 2020, as lockdowns spread across the globe, anthropologists – and particularly student anthropologists – came face-to-face with a new reality: anthropology without in-person fieldwork. Thousands of trips were canceled, dissertation proposals re-tooled, and grants either lost or deferred. Colleagues who had just begun their work were forced to pack up and leave – erasing months of preparation in the process. Could there be an anthropology without fieldwork? Perhaps, many people asked, digital fieldwork could substitute (Collins and Durington 2020)? The problem, here, is this word "substitute"; digital anthropology is a form of ethnographic inquiry in its own right, and attempts to simply map face-to-face fieldwork onto a digital environment are doomed in the same way that efforts to teach face-to-face classes online are doomed: both are made of up affordances and practices that cannot be reproduced in the other. Moving your interviews to Zoom is, of course, possible, but that is not the digitization of face-to-face interviews; the two are very different and, unsurprisingly, the experience of interviews via Zoom differs in many ways from face-to-face encounters (Laughlin et al. 2022). And yet – even if they wanted to replace one with the other – many other people have not been able to engage in digital fieldwork. Or, to put it another way, the turn to digital fieldwork has enabled some anthropologies while rendering others nearly impossible. With many still not able to access digital tools in their everyday life, many of the populations traditionally researched in anthropology are effectively invisible in digital anthropology. Of course, none of this is new; as Rivera-González et al. (2022: 291) remind us:

> COVID-19 as a revelatory crisis is a misleading dialogue, as the problems highlighted by the pandemic did not reveal anything novel to those who previously experienced disenfranchisement. Instead, the pandemic offered continuations or transformations of existing issues, leaving those affected to turn to existing pre-pandemic self- and community-constructed solutions to navigate long-standing problems.

DOI: 10.4324/9781003443735-1

2 *Introduction*

The "novelty" here, such as it is, is the inability of anthropologists to engage communities in any other modality than the digital – a method that throws the deep inequalities of anthropology into bold relief. And paradoxically, by facilitating some forms of fieldwork, the move to digital fieldwork since the pandemic has resulted in even more marginalization and invisibility for people in many communities where anthropologists have worked.

On the one hand, these are clearly the effects of a digital divide. On the other, outside of the pandemic, we can imagine many other ways of accomplishing anthropology that do not compound digital divides, yet still are very imbricated in power and inequality with respect to institutions, cultural capital, and other forms of gatekeeping. As we explore below, this is neither to exonerate digital approaches nor is it an attempt to naturalize inequality. What this has underscored, of course, is that the multimodal can give us a variety of perspectives; it can engage people in different ways, yet these forms of engagement bring different inequalities to the fore.

Another legacy of the pandemic has been the way it's focused attention on the inequalities of anthropology and the ways that our work is complicit in those inequalities. At the 2021 American Anthropological Association Annual Meeting in Baltimore, Akhil Gupta outlined a comprehensive vision of what a decolonized anthropology would look like, from multiple perspectives: in research, in teaching, in departments. Multimodal anthropology – as we've outlined it here – addresses many of those concerns. First, methodologically. "How do the methods that we use enable or constrain decolonization? What kinds of methods, collaborative practices, etc., might be needed to shape anthropology in a decolonizing science?" (Gupta and Stoolman 2022: 786). While we make the case here that multimodality is no panacea for anthropology's ills, it does highlight the powerful inequalities that shape ethnographic practice. Above all else, multimodal anthropology must strive for collaboration, and collaboration entails ethical labor. Again, while doing collaborative work is in itself no guarantee of a transformed anthropology, it multiplies the opportunities for interrogating anthropology's colonial past.

Second, multimodal anthropology raises the possibility of not just different research, but research that belongs to a collaborative community rather than the anthropologist-as-auteur. Gupta and Stoolman ask, for example, "what rights should the people we study have in and about our scholarship?" (Gupta and Stoolman 2022: 786). Distributed across analog and digital media, and representing the collaborative efforts of many, multimodal anthropology calls into question the fiction of the "lone anthropologist," the Conrad-esque character who extracts cultural knowledge from the colonized.

Part of the challenge of a truly decolonized anthropology is to imagine a field that may in some ways be no longer recognizable as anthropology – at least from the perspective of the liberal anthropology of the 20th century. This means an anthropology that is different in every respect, from who "counts" as an anthropologist, to the ways that ethnography is practiced and disseminated, to the whole rationale for research in the first place. At least some of the provocation behind Jobson's abjuration to "let anthropology burn" is precisely the promise (and, to some, the threat) that anthropology will no longer be recognizable as such, and that its colonial origins – while still salient to our understanding – will be utterly transformed into something more equitable and, even, more hopeful (Jobson 2020). Transformed from its colonial past, such an anthropology may work for justice and equity rather than for book contracts and academic promotions. What that looks like in terms of faculty, students, and departments is difficult to predict. Yet multimodal anthropology may offer some glimpse in the valuation of expertise beyond the anthropologist, in the insistence that anthropological inquiry can take place through many different platforms, and in contexts where the anthropologist is more of a placeholder than a person.

You and Multimodality

You may have come across this book for a variety of reasons, and we have written this volume with several uses and several audiences in mind. First, we mean it as an introductory grounding in multimodality as a collaborative method of anthropological inquiry extending across different platforms. Yet as we discuss below, we do not mean to imply that this is a "break" with the past of anthropology. It is, as we write in the initial chapter, an opportunity to confront the history of the field in new and productive ways, to realize the potentials and pitfalls of media among some of the earliest practitioners of anthropology as well as in some of anthropology's most recent work.

What does it mean to begin doing multimodal anthropology in your own work? First and foremost, it means working with people to produce things that fit their purposes and advance their goals. In itself, that is a big shift from the way anthropology has ordinarily been undertaken. Typically, anthropologists shape their research from interesting questions or gaps in the literature. Both of us began our careers like this, and, on the surface, there is nothing wrong with this approach. After all, this is how most empirical research works. Yet even if community approval has been sought as part of the proposal process, it has been the researcher that has initiated the work. Reversing that – beginning with the goals and needs of people – is, of course, a familiar strategy in applied and collaborative anthropology, but it is less common with anthropologists producing multimedia. In media production the notion of the auteur and their vision is paramount and there is usually a crew hierarchy, funding and a structure that centralizes power to one individual… the filmmaker, media producer, or author will impart what the community may want or need by representing them. And this is not to minimize the difficulty in deciding what the community wants and needs; multimodal anthropology as we've defined it is going to involve continued negotiations across a charged field.

Second, it means collaborating with others. Although anthropological fieldwork has been a team endeavor since its inception in the late 19th century, the ideology of the lone ethnographer lives on in the anthropological canon and, more importantly, in graduate training, where the status quo is still for an individual proposal followed by one to two years of individual fieldwork (Marcus 2008). But we make the case in this volume that multimodal anthropology is an inherently collaborative project. At the very least, few of us possess the multiple competencies to engage in broad, multimodal work. Between photos, film, illustration, games, and apps, one would have to have manifold talents to be able to utilize all of them. In fact, some people do. We do not. Moreover, the point here is to work with communities on media that would be useful to them – in other words, a collaborative effort.

Finally, undertaking multimodal anthropology means extending what we mean by "ethnography" and "anthropology." The history of visual anthropology is bound up with the battle to establish film as a bonafide medium for anthropological research (Hockings 1995). The success of that fight has been admirable, with visual anthropology taking its place alongside other forms of ethnographic practice (see Postscript). Our hope, however, is that multimodal anthropology remains an enigmatic "boundary object" that may bring people together in different ways that may remain problematic or even contentious (Star 2010). Even more than this, we hope that multimodal anthropology continues to straddle the boundary between what we "count" as anthropology and what we locate as outside of the field. Perhaps multimodal anthropology might work to destabilize the canon altogether! This could work both ways – anthropologists might engage in multimodal work that pushes the envelope on what it means to be an anthropologist, while people in the communities where we work might engage in something that is for all intents and purposes anthropological, and that works to challenge the inequalities in cultures of "expertise" that delimit policymaking to an elite group while minimizing the contributions of citizens. Whatever direction this takes, the goal is to make anthropology more relevant to the world and more responsive to its injustices. If it, however, becomes merely another canonical theory taking its place among other subfields and theories, then structures of authority will probably persist into the future.

Accordingly, our hope is that this volume proves a catalyst for your own work. As we argue in the Conclusion, a healthy future for multimodal anthropology is one where developments are surprising and stochastic – one where anthropologists and their collaborators explore a widening ambit of media possibilities. Not, however, just new media, but the many possibilities that already exist in this mediated world. And, as we hope for our students, our desire in writing this book is for people to exceed what we have done here, and to develop multimodal anthropology in ways that we have scarcely anticipated.

Explanation of Chapters

The first chapter in the book attempts to discuss the past, present and future of multimodal anthropology. We discuss historical antecedents that inform a formulation of multimodal anthropology from past projects and figures in the discipline. We also revisit our time as the inaugural editors of the multimodal anthropologies section in *American Anthropologist* starting in 2017 and the intentionality behind the work we solicited for this burgeoning part of our practice. Multimodal anthropology is not necessarily unique and by visiting the history and present of what we are discussing as multimodal anthropology we hope to show some of the novel work taking place and point toward further work. We also position a "rogue's gallery" of multimodal anthropologists and discuss the historical and contemporary importance of collaboration, tools and how they inform multimodal work.

The second chapter, "Old Questions and New Directions," develops the ethical implications of multimodality as, in many ways, a reprise of ethical problems in anthropology in general. Or, more accurately, the ethical problems in multimodal anthropology are familiar because anthropology is above all else an ethical inquiry, one premised on forming relationships with people. While those relationships have often been one-sided and even exploitative, they are, nevertheless, human relations that we can subject to ethical examination. And although we hope anthropology has become less exploitative over time, we still find those relationships at the core of the field. What multimodal anthropology does, however, is make certain ethical orientations more explicit, throwing, for example, power relations relating to digital divides into bold relief.

From there, the chapters explore different media engagements from multimodal perspectives, with each chapter returning to one of the core tenets of this volume, that multimodal anthropology is above all else a collaborative agreement that continuously challenges us to confront inequalities both within the fieldwork encounter and without – in society as a whole. It's worth noting that there is no pretense here that each of these chapters exhausts their subjects. Photography, mapping, apps, etc.: each of these mediums develops across decades of ethnographic work. Multimodality here is a provocation, an extension of these into contexts that are revelatory of new or transformed possibility.

The third chapter explores ramifications of a multimodal photography. Photography provides many opportunities for multimodal anthropology. Photography is considered the oldest representational medium in anthropology beyond written notes and drawings. Photography is a space to consider the tensions between text and image theoretically. The practice also bears evidence to the colonial roots of the discipline and the unequal relations between anthropologists and their interlocutors historically. Photography was meant to provide empirical proof of *in situ* fieldwork and represent the anthropological encounter. Yet, photography also infamously misrepresents. Anthropologists have utilized photography in participatory action research practices such as photovoice and as a tool for photo elicitation.

The fourth chapter considers mapping, taking it from its colonialist, extractive origins to a collaborative, communicative media capable of not just documenting the relationship to place, but of critiquing the reduction of place to commodities. The chapter summarizes these possibilities in three case studies, but also (and as with all multimodal work) sounds a cautionary note. Collaborative, multimodal anthropology, undertaken with communities in the spirit of critique, can just as easily become subsumed into the urban "growth machine." Local attachments to place can re-emerge as "local charm"; local histories as stops on a "heritage trail," and social justice as value-added murals painted by neighborhood outsiders.

The fifth chapter continues this discussion into the world of games. Games are arguably the most multimodal of media, yet, paradoxically, have been relatively infrequently utilized by anthropology – despite the historical salience of games for our understanding of culture. This chapter hopes to remedy that by presenting games in three contexts: in teaching, in ethnographic research, and, finally, in ethnography itself. As we have seen through a series of "AnthropologyCon" events held at successive American Anthropological Association Annual Meetings, there is a good deal of interest in games in anthropology, and we would expect this to be a growth area in multimodal work. In addition, it's worth noting that many indie games have been published that are altogether anthropological in their approach.

In the sixth chapter, we turn to a related platform: apps. Apps have become ubiquitous (although not always acknowledged) in anthropological research. They also represent a multimodal opportunity to collaborate with communities of people. After all, we have been asked many times to help people "make an app" that will allow them to accomplish their goals. Yet while apps may be a fixture in much of contemporary life around the world, they are also a "black box" with regards to their programming, design, and, as we argue, their "back-end" maintenance. So while much of our work with communities on creating apps has involved dissuading them from making an app (for reasons we explain), it's clear that they represent a flashpoint in our multimodal work, and they stand at the confluence of our collaboration with communities, designers, programmers, and student ethnographers.

In the seventh chapter, we end our survey of multimodal engagement with a discussion of design anthropology. Over the last three decades, what we now call design anthropology anticipates many of the insights we've cultivated through our multimodal work. It always involves groups of people working together through a variety of media to create something. On the other hand, design anthropology has oftentimes been yoked to the creation of new commodities through UX (user experience) research. In this chapter, we wrestle with that legacy while outlining a design anthropology that is, in the end, about the evocation of other possibilities, a "speculative anthropology" that is nevertheless grounded in community goals and collaborative work (Salazar 2017).

What We Haven't Covered

Multimodal anthropology is continuously unfolding as people reflect on their ethnographic practice and build more collaborative work engaging people across multiple media. These chapters are moments in that open-ended process of becoming and revelation. The corollary to this is that this text is also punctuated by absences – ethnographic modes that we have not explored here, in addition to all of the multimodalities yet to come. Our reasons for omissions are both theoretical and quotidian. Some of these (film) are so much of a part of our understanding of media that we felt that a chapter on visual anthropology would hardly be revelatory, given the many monographs on that very subject over the past several decades. We provide some guideposts for understanding ethnographic film by burgeoning multimodal anthropologists in our postscript. Other absences speak more to our own interests and talents. In any case, we believe that these are still at the heart of multimodality, and they represent areas that we hope to explore in our future work. Here are a few of these:

Drawing and illustration. There is a very long history of drawing and illustration in anthropology and archaeology, one that even extends after the invention of portable cameras and half-tone printing. The natural sciences develop through sketches – of flora, fauna, people, and artifacts. From Darwin's sketchbook on the Galapagos to Torres Straits drawings, to Spencer's and Gillen's notes on the Arrernte, drawing and illustration are methods that prove more revelatory in some respects than the photographs and films that were rapidly becoming the dominant multimedia in anthropological fieldwork.

In particular, drawings could be rendered by community collaborators, as Boas and Hunt did throughout the Pacific Northwest (Glass 2018). Haddon's Torres Straits teams commissioned drawings from Torres Strait Islanders as part of their "salvage" anthropology into reconstructions of culture before the arrival of missionaries, and the archived work still affords insights into Torres Strait aesthetics and historical memory (Brady 2012). Eventually, the ubiquity of cameras and the ease of half-tone reproduction led to the near-absence of drawing and illustration in 20th century anthropology (although not, importantly, in archaeology). Over the past 20 years, however, drawing and illustration have made a remarkable recovery in anthropology. As Ingold (2010: 2) urges at the beginning of this re-birth, anthropologists should "think of drawing not just as a means to illustrate an otherwise written text, but as an inscriptive practice in its own right." These multimodal methods represent a different way of seeing, doing, and connection – in short, a robust ethnographic practice that represents an intimate interface between people and place, one whose revelations are entirely different from other visual media. "Sitting and looking at a familiar object, such as the clock on the mantelpiece or the door one has entered a thousand times, makes it strange" (Hurdley et al. 2017: 750).

Exhibits. Much of the energy that has animated multimodal anthropology in the United States over the past several years stems from a moment of ethnographic experimentation – the Ethnographic Terminalia project. Before that, however, the history of exhibits goes back to the very beginnings of the field – to, for example, the foundation of the Pitt Rivers Museum, and to the Bureau of American Ethnology and the Smithsonian Institution (Woodbury and Woodbury 1999). Museum anthropology is a very robust and viable subfield, and includes within it many multimodal elements concerning display and the politics of representation. Of course, what we mean by "exhibit" is both more and less than this; communities may display photographs, video, or other media that represent place or that develop an argument about resources or other community issues. Is a photovoice exhibit about one's neighborhood the same thing as an exhibit in a museum? On the level of practice, they seem very different – a photo exhibit in a community center, a gallery, and a museum are all doing different things. Perhaps what ties them together is the attention to audience and interaction; exhibits are made to be seen by particular people in particular contexts.

Performance. Performance and performance studies have long histories in anthropology. Yet these, like other examples of multimodality, have often been passed over in anthropology's relentless textuality. That said, anthropologists like Elizabeth Chin have developed performance into a devastatingly critical anthropology that brings together theory and practice and that also serves as a springboard for other, plastic arts (e.g., costume design and art installations). Similarly, as Kondo and others have shown, theater allows anthropologists to collaborate on the evocations of other worlds and engage in a level of critique that facilitates the articulation of intersections of power and identity in ways that would not be as possible in more static and atemporal media. As Kondo (2018: 26) notes, "Theater gathers bodies, both performers and audience, who share space and time, affecting and being affected by each other. This copresence possesses the potential for forming temporary communities." One of us (Durington) has engaged in just this sort of performative practice, with his role as Stewart Brand in a dramatization of the 1976 "trialogue" between Brand, Gregory Bateson, and Margaret Mead. By interspersing Balinese performance in the interstices of the debate over cameras and their capacity to illuminate culture, and by engaging the audience at various levels in question and answer, tensions between reflexivity and fieldwork, between community and media, and, ultimately, about the role of anthropology in the world itself could be explored (Cool 2020).

References

Brady, L. (2012). Adding value. *Visual Anthropology*, 25, 167–188.
Collins, S.G., & Durington, M.S. (2020). The case for letting anthropology be quarantined: COVID and the end of ethnographic presence. *Entanglements*, 3(2), 92–96.

Cool, J. (2020). Tripod. *American Anthropologist*, 122(3), 684–690.
Glass, A. (2018). Drawing on museums. *American Anthropologist*, 120(1), 72–88.
Gupta, A., & Stoolman, J. (2022). Decolonizing US anthropology. *American Anthropologist*, 124(4), 778–799.
Hockings, P. (ed.) (1995). *Principles of visual anthropology*. De Gruyter.
Hurdley, R., Biddulph, M., Backhaus, V., Hipwood, T., & Hossain, R. (2017). Drawing as radical multimodality: Salvaging Patrick Geddes's material methodology. *American Anthropologist*, 119, 748–753. https://doi.org/10.1111/aman.12963.
Ingold, T. (2010). Ways of mind-walking: Reading, writing, painting. *Visual Studies*, 25(1), 15–23.
Jobson, R.C. (2020). The case for letting anthropology burn. *American Anthropologist*, 122(2), 259–271.
Kondo, D. (2018). *World-making*. Duke University Press.
Laughlin, T.G., Deep, A., Prichard, A.M.*et al*. (2022). Architecture and self-assembly of the jumbo bacteriophage nuclear shell. *Nature*, 608, 429–435. https://doi.org/10.1038/s41586-022-05013-4.
Marcus, G.E. (2008). Collaborative options and pedagogical experiment in anthropological research on experts and policy processes. *Anthropology in Action*, 15(2), 47–57. https://doi.org/10.3167/aia.2008.150205.
Rivera-González, J., Trivedi, J., Marino, E.K., & Dietrich, A. (2020). Imagining an ethnographic otherwise during a pandemic. *Human Organization*, 81(3), 291–300.
Salazar, J.F. (2017). Speculative fabulation. In J. Salazar, S. Pink, A. Irving, & J. Sjoberg (eds), *Anthropologies and futures*. Routledge, pp. 151–170.
Star, S.L. (2010). This is not a boundary object. *Science, Technology, & Human Values*, 35(3), 601–617.
Woodbury, R.B., & Woodbury, N.F.S. (1999). The rise and fall of the Bureau of American Ethnology. *Journal of the Southwest*, 41(3), 283–296.

1 Multimodality

Multimodality is about the platforms we use as we produce our work (social media, blogs, websites), and the social media that ripple out from them as people share, comment, remix, and appropriate. Finally, multimodality is the acknowledgement that people are engaged in anthropologies of their own lives, and that these productions (YouTube videos, Instagram photos) are worthy of attention as ethnographically intended media in their own rights. By multimodality, then, we recognize anthropology along two complementary axes – a horizontal one that links together phases of anthropological research that are oftentimes held distinct from each other, and a vertical one that links our anthropological work to the anthropologies of our collaborators. Moreover, with the development of new media, new media platforms, and new forms of collaborative work, we have seen these axes multiply. Ultimately, multimodality takes the arbitrary divisions we make in our work and in our collaborations to task, and offers up new possibilities for old dilemmas. This presents exciting possibilities for ethnographic media production and creates new emergent works, partnerships, and audiences. To the point of this book, anthropology has been multimodal for quite some time we will argue. But the recognition and academic validation of a multimodal anthropology started in the US in 2017.

As editor of the flagship journal for the discipline of anthropology in the United States, Deborah Thomas made the bold step of rebranding the "Visual Anthropology" section of *American Anthropologist* to "Multimodal Anthropologies." This was not simply a renaming, but a reconceptualization and call for visual anthropology to start a critical discussion of inclusivity, technology changes, and collaboration, to name a few. The main principle building on work at the University of Pennsylvania by Dr. Thomas and her students was to open up possibilities. While some colleagues in visual anthropology were dismayed by the rebranding, we worked diligently to bring in as many forms of what could be considered multimodal work as possible. As we detail throughout the book, we want to create more opportunities for collaboration by centering it as the principal component of a multimodal anthropology. In addition to collaborative possibilities created by a multimodal anthropology we also want to disrupt the commonly held

DOI: 10.4324/9781003330851-2

exotification of the solo anthropologist in the field and recognize the process of ethnographic work. We also proceed with caution as our colleagues have warned of technological determinism.

In "Bad Habitus: Anthropology in the Age of the Multimodal," our colleagues Stephanie Takaragawa, Trudi Smith, Kate Hennessey, Patricia Alvarez Astacio, Jenny Chio, Coleman Nye, and Shalini Shakar question the potential liberatory and democratic possibilities of a multimodal approach in the discipline:

> Although the idea of multimodal anthropology may challenge dominant paradigms of authorship, expertise, capacity, and language, we argue that there is nothing inherently liberatory about multimodal approaches in anthropology. Therefore, as our discipline(s) increasingly advocates for the multimodal in the service of anthropology, there is a need for deep engagement with the multimodal's position as an expression of technoscientific praxis, which is complicit in the reproduction of power hierarchies in the context of global capitalism, "capital accumulation"… and other forms of oppression.
> (Takaragawa et al. 2019: 517)

We could not agree more with this sentiment.

Thus, multimodal anthropology is not unique. It may not even be innovative. We will make several claims along these lines throughout this book. Multimodality has been around as long as anthropology. Just because a new technology, recording device, platform, or mode of analysis comes along does not mean that the field of anthropology is undergoing a tectonic shift. If that was the case, then the pencil and paper were the most technologically deterministic tools ever invented. Multimodality is trapped tautologically if it is solely based on the new fun tool in our toolbox. Multimodality involves new tools and new tools create multimodality. It is therefore it is. New devices are interesting if not fun to explore as we conduct ethnographic fieldwork, produce work, and, as an ethical necessity, enter into collaborative work with our interlocutors. As we will continue to emphasize, if one is not collaborative in their work and its dissemination, then one is not practicing or producing multimodal anthropology. Multimodality can be dangerous and replicate the colonial vestiges of the discipline historically. It can also be disruptive alongside other critical takes on the field that have come before the term became somewhat popular in this discipline.

Readers may also notice that multimodal anthropology is also a process of reclamation of historical precedents. And we would assert that anyone making a claim of originality, particularly because of a new technology, may be hiding something. We wanted to ask these questions many times as editors particularly if something appeared incomplete and may have had a different intended purpose. Oh, you never finished your film? Your play sucks but you want to emphasize the process? You are not an artist, sorry. Your music is tired, that's why it's not getting the attention you think it should. Also, where is your collaborator?

In 2017, we defined "multimodality" as "not only an anthropology that works across multiple media but one that also engages in public anthropology and collaborative anthropology through a field of differentially linked media platforms." Many claims to multimodal work more often than not serve as a stand-in for multimedia. Vannini writes about multimodal practices in ethnography:

> Traditional ethnographies are for the most part unimodal, that is, they are communication products that make use of only one mode of communication: writing. Gesturing and singing are other modes, and so is writing. Television is a single medium, but it can transmit several modes of communication such as recorded or live dialog, still images, moving images, and writing. There are multiple and growing possibilities for combining ethnographic writing with other modes for different analytical purposes or for the sake of broader knowledge mobilization. Whether a journal is published in HTML or PDF version, photos and video can be embedded directly into one's writing. While photography needs writing to convey a more contextualized message, video is immediately multimodal when it conveys multiple forms of communication such as speech, gesture, movement, and other sounds.
>
> (Vannini 2019)

It's certainly true that a multimedia approach to ethnography represents many forms of communication. What Vaninni is really describing here is an ethnographic product with different forms of communication. In some sense, it could be deemed multimodal but then what is not multimodal? Therefore, a more robust approach to multimodal work is one that is guided by a particular ethics, methodology, collaboration, critical consciousness of power dynamics, and can take a variety of novel forms approaching unique phenomena. Any discussion or definition of multimodal anthropology should explicitly address these factors and the product or form of dissemination might actually be the last thing to consider.

Launched in 2021, the journal *Multimodality & Society* seeks to bring together some of the diverse strands of multimodality ranging from linguistics to film studies and beyond. The journal has also explored multimodality as a more explicit practice, as in this contribution from Gupta:

> In this essay, I propose a multimodal way to convey shifting urban landscapes of memory, one embedded in the conversations and affordances of varied media and methods, including mapping, video, poetry, photography, material artifacts, and collaborative fieldwork.

Multimodality here derives from feminist, decolonial practice that seeks to unsettle linear temporality and the protocols of scientific argumentation...

(Gupta 2021: 282)

In the essay Gupta pursues non-linear forms of representation in order to undermine the colonialist discourse of urban development in India. There is also a genealogical link to anthropology's "experimental moment," as Marcus and Fischer called their 1986 book, *Anthropology as Cultural Critique* (Marcus and Fischer 1986). Finally, multimodal approaches offer Gupta an opportunity to contribute to a "world-making" enterprise that pits this alternative representation of urban life and history against developmental discourse, what the author calls a "speculative urbanism as a future-oriented transformation that is present and ongoing, navigated through lived experience and knowable through an embodied, affective, situated feminist multimodality" (Gupta 2021: 287).

There are two conclusions here. One, that "multimodality" (standing alone) is not itself a political practice – hence Gupta's invocation of feminist and decolonial methods. At the same time, though, the qualifier is required; this is a "feminist multimodality." To us, this passage underlines the chief tension in multimodal methods. Simply producing media in the course of ethnographic fieldwork and pitting those media against each other in some form of dissemination does not in itself imply multimodality. There is, as we have outlined above, a long history of multimedia research in anthropology, one that we argue cannot be unproblematically called "multimodal." And, yet, what is that difference? Why does Gupta need to qualify this research as a "feminist" and "decolonial" multimodality? Would it mean the same thing here to write a "feminist multimedia"?

There are at least two characteristics that differentiate "multimodality" from "multimedia." First, "multimodality" describes a process, one indissolubly linked to fieldwork and community engagement. "Multimedia," on the other hand, merely describes a collection of outcomes – the visual, the aural, the textual. As we describe below, multimodality focuses attention on a collaborative process, one that can be structured by a deeply participatory ethos. Of course, it doesn't have to be, and there are many works that have been labeled "multimodal" that are not especially participatory, or that, on the contrary, are top-down productions redolent of a more colonial anthropology.

Rather, and this brings us to our second point, describing one's work as "multimodal" begs the question of power and collaboration. It focuses attention on the process of fieldwork, from the construction of fieldsites to the dissemination of multimodal materials and their afterlives in the churn of internet appropriations. When Astacio, Dattatreyan, and Shankar took over as editors for the multimodal section in the *American Anthropologist*, they sought to "embrace an ambivalence towards its promise and potential and to offer an invitation for you to do the same" (Astacio et al. 2021: 241). That "ambivalence" extends from skepticism about the democratizing potential of digital technologies and from the colonial trappings of an anthropology that too often adopts new methods and theories as a form of virtue signaling while, underneath, the status quo prevails and the next generation of anthropologists lays their knowledge claims to "their" fieldsites.

However, it is difficult to think of any element of anthropological research without considerable ambivalence (Jobson 2020). Rather, we see multimodality as highlighting the contradictions of media and technology alongside the colonial past of the discipline. With text, these ambivalences are, of course, still there, but are concealed and uncontested in a graphocentric world. When people write about the "digital divide," they ordinarily refer to the highly unequal distribution of information technologies like smartphones and computers. Yet not only are academic journals invisible to most general internet searches, but the articles themselves are paywalled and really only accessible to other academics. This is a profound divide, one that underscores deep inequalities in knowledge and access.

The difference here is that multimodal works confront ideologies of democratization that accompany the development of digital technologies, the "computopian" promises for increased access and participation that have followed every new IT product since the IBM 360 (Hakken and Andrews 1993). As hollow as these ideologies are, they nevertheless raise the question of inequality; with new technologies, questions immediately revolve around barriers to access. This is, we submit, one of the advantages of multimodality. Spread between multiple media and distributed through different communities, multimodality always begs the question of access and equality, and multimodal methods are a foil against which to measure a number of structural inequalities. One of the first responses to the invitation to contribute to the multimodal section of *American Anthropologist* upon its rebranding and redirection was a critique by colleagues following the traditional jousting of academia, i.e. throw out a new idea and watch as others attempt to eviscerate it and perhaps develop it further. While this critical approach to multimodality is welcomed of course, it elides the fact that the grounding of a multimodal approach is an interrogation of its embeddedness in global capitalism and technological determinism.

When Takaragawa et al. critique multimodality in anthropology as "complicit in the reproduction of power hierarchies in the context of global capitalism," they are, therefore, entirely justified (Takaragawa et al. 2019: 518). From the exploitative production of information technologies and their highly unequal distribution, to their differently networked, differently valued and differently monetized content, the information technologies that underlie much of multimodality are flashpoints for inequality. At the same time, these ideologies of access make their inequalities more visible. For example, Facebook and WhatsApp usage is widespread in many countries, especially India and Brazil. People in both of these countries are much more likely to access the internet with their phones, and it is not surprising that Facebook and WhatsApp (which is owned by Facebook) have been virtually synonymous with the internet. As Nerner reports, "To many favela residents, Facebook was the internet. In other words, Facebook dominated their online experience. Most teenagers and older adults were not aware of non-Facebook services and couldn't tell which online services were outside Facebook's boundaries" (Nerner 2022: 83). The availability of relatively inexpensive smartphones, and the efforts of Facebook to capture working-class Brazilians with a "zero-rating" plan, allowed them to use Facebook apps for free on their phones (Nerner 2022: 84).

Multimodality is more than the sum of its multimedia. It also recognizes that media platforms are differently networked to different publics in a variety of contexts. This can mean "live fieldnoting" your work on Instagram (Wang 2012; Powis 2017), utilizing Facebook or other platforms to organize a photo exhibition (Dattatreyan 2015), reciprocating with YouTube users through your own video commentary (Markham 2012), or, in a platform that predates "social media" *per se*, blogging the struggles and negotiations of fieldwork (Saka 2008). In all cases, the advantages are similar: 1) immediate feedback from colleagues and interlocutors; 2) increased visibility and transparency through readily accessible, public platforms; and 3) the opportunity for new contacts in the field and/or at home. The concerns are also similar. As we have discussed at some length (Collins and Durington 2014), the networked visibility of social media is simultaneously its biggest drawback with regards to ethics, the confidentiality of interlocutors, and the desires anthropologists and interlocutors have to present data in the context within which they were intended. However, as Powis (2017: 360) points out, the ethical questions raised by social media are equally applicable to print – especially digital print, which, like its more "social" counterpart, has more and more incorporated socially networked affordances.

Moreover, these social media platforms are, for anthropologists, merely the latest iterations of long-standing communications between fieldworkers, interlocutors, and colleagues. These include the letters, correspondence, and reciprocities that have long been at the heart of fieldwork, even though the importance of these networked communications has long been suppressed in the stories anthropologists tell themselves. Post-war anthropology in the US and Europe was dominated by images of the "anthropologist as hero" (Sontag 1966), only to be replaced in anthropology's "postmodern turn" by a more supine (but no less heroic) "anthropologist as author." Both are deeply imbricated in the racialized, gendered production of anthropological knowledge and both leave ethnographic authority intact by elevating the production of text over the vicissitudes of a highly negotiated fieldsite and, in the process, re-inscribing colonial relations through the production of anthropological knowledge. But the anthropologist and the anthropologist's fieldnotes are only two highly fetishized objects in a much more complex field of relations and exchanges.

Ultimately, though, the turn to social media offers a path toward a more public, more collaborative anthropology. What we see in projects such as Karen Waltrop's work among immigrants to Denmark is precisely this robust sense of social media as not only a tool for data collection, but as a platform for collaboration and, ultimately, an opportunity for the co-production of ethnographic work (Waltrop 2017: 103). In other words, fieldwork unfolding both on social media and through social media. In actuality, the choice is not whether or not to utilize social media in one's research: meeting people "where they are" requires that we use the same communication platforms they use, platforms that more and more of us have grown up with. The real question is whether or not to acknowledge our embeddedness in networked social media. And not just in the sense of the "return of the repressed," as when the publication of Malinowski's *Diary in the Strict Sense* precipitated a guilty interrogation of anthropology's entrenched colonialism, misogyny, and racism, but with the goal of creating a collaborative, co-temporal space for ethnographic work that may make a difference in the lives of people in the communities where we work.

The next part of this chapter reclaims some of the history of anthropology as inherently multimodal. The present, we assert, is less of a "departure" or a "break" than a return to anthropological work that has been interrupted by disciplinary siloing and by print capitalism. Next, we look at what has been occurring in the field, why it is important, why you should be using it, and how it opens up a critique of the field. This discussion opens the door for how to practice multimodal methods and the ethics of this work. We emphasize that a multimodal approach still necessitates core elements of anthropology such as rapport building and that one cannot forego these grounding methods ethically and methodologically.

Our Multimodal Past, Reclaiming Anthropology as Multimodal

A nascent multimodality shows up in 20th century anthropology mapped onto each technological development that pushed ethnographic modalities forward – again, proceeding with a modicum of caution to not be technologically deterministic. Part of the multimodal project is a reflection back onto missed opportunities and potentialities from the history of anthropology. In this sense, the multimodal becomes multitemporal as each new possibility realized by interactions with technology by anthropologists triggers a need to look back in the annals of the discipline for individuals who foregrounded these possibilities. This is particularly important when anthropologists have demonstrated both a willingness and ethos to regard the populations they work with as collaborators in the production of knowledge and the process of fieldwork. There are rare occasions where these progenitors have included these collaborators in authorship, and when they do it demonstrates the true nature of multimodal work that encourages partnership.

In the era of "armchair anthropology," correspondence was the primary tool for research, what Stocking has called "epistolary ethnography" (Stocking 1984: 6). Without his voluminous correspondence, Tylor would never had been able to collect artifacts for the Pitt-Rivers museum, nor would he had been able to slot these artifacts into his erroneous typologies representing other people along a sliding scale of racial, ethnic, and class inferiority vis-à-vis white, (northern) European men. Many of the letters Tylor received from his professional correspondents refer to an object or objects solicited by him, or give contextual information concerning an item already acquired regarding its use and meanings, as understood by the collector among the source community. These letters contain rich descriptions about the functions of objects, often including indigenous terminology and secondary information concerning how each object was procured. Some letters contain sketches or diagrams, and occasionally photographs illustrating the object in use (Brown et al. 2000: 267–268).

In the decades before the professionalization of fieldwork, Tylor's livelihood not only depended upon these exchanges, but developed through them. The monographs through which we understand this period (*Primitive Culture, The Golden Bough*) were but islands in an endless stream of correspondence linking researchers with a dense skein of travelers, colonial administrators, and collectors all over the world. But the emergence of fieldwork was itself enabled through correspondence. Spencer's and Gillen's work among Arrernte peoples was productive of a very rich correspondence, as was the Torres Straits expedition, Griaule's Dakar-Djibouti expedition, and many others (Petch 2006). Historians of anthropology have often utilized correspondence in order to contextualize work and writing, but comparatively little has been written about letter writing *qua* ethnographic methodology (Cerwonka and Malkki 2008).

Not all anthropologists have downplayed the importance of networks of correspondence. As, perhaps, one of the last great correspondents of the 20th century Margaret Mead wrote much more than occasional missives to her family and friends. Letters *drove* her fieldwork and served as fora for theoretical provocations, as well as a catalyst to her ever expanding ambit of networked connections. It was not egocentricity that led Mead to keep carbon copies of most of her (typed) correspondence. She knew their value. Moreover, consonant with her interest in cybernetics, Mead was also conscious of the power of the platform itself to shape the content of communication (Collins 2008). When she was working with Gregory Bateson in Papua New Guinea in the early 1930s, she would correspond with small slips of paper sent back and forth by messenger: "Designed for recording fieldnotes, these specially-sized pieces of paper facilitated, piece by piece, an ongoing intimate conversation of personal, logistical and anthropological issues" (Caffrey and Francis 2009: xxvi). Not surprisingly, Mead was an early adopter of technologies for scholarly communication, including both the telephone and reel-to-reel recordings. In fact, her prodigious production of correspondence only began to abate with her investment in telephony before her championing of an anthropology of visual communication and visual anthropology.

As a platform, it would be hard to find something more essential to anthropological work than the telephone. Talking to colleagues, to interlocutors, to grantors, to publishers: anthropological work from the mid-twentieth century until the present emerges in the interstices of telephone work. But there is little acknowledgement of the telephone in discussions of anthropological methods, a curious lacunae Sunderland notes in a 1999 article:

> Not only were some of my deepest friendships forged and some of my intimate conversations with women of the community carried out over the phone, many of my telephone conversations were participant observation realized in one of its idealized forms.
>
> (Sunderland 1999: 106)

This leads Sunderland to call for the acknowledgement of telephone practices in ethnographic methodology: "It is about time that we included them, and admitted to including them, as integral parts of our fieldwork" (Sunderland 1999: 115).

This resistance to acknowledging the embeddedness of anthropological fieldwork in telephony is not just from fieldwork ideologies that elevate the importance of face-to-face encounters over other forms of communication; it also comes from the insistence on anthropological methods as distinct from quotidian life. The "field" is constructed according to degrees of difference, and the stereotyped tools of anthropology – notebook, typewriter – are exceptional documentary practices that literally remove the fieldworker from the *mise-en-scène* in order to engage their anthropological practice. But it all becomes a good deal messier if "field" and "home," "familiar" and "strange," aren't seen as dichotomous, but as deeply interpenetrated fields of practice.

And if this is true of the telephone, how much more the case for the smartphone? With global adoption rates ticking up to nearly 50%, many of anthropology's interlocutors (and especially younger ones) utilize smartphones to do the same things anthropologists do: keep in contact with friends, set up appointments, share ideas and media content. This has only accelerated with text messaging in the 21st century where one becomes irritated if they receive a telephone call on their actual telephone. If we acknowledge that much of our fieldwork looks similar to the things people do every day, what do we lose? Something of the mystique and the pretense to anthropological exceptionalism, doubtless. That said, anthropologists still bear the onus to work within ethical frames that include working to confront power – but here, we are frequently not so different from our interlocutors as well.

As any competent ethnographic documentary filmmaker will impart, one of the most important things to consider when creating film or video is sound. One can be the most accomplished aesthetician or auteur, but if synchronous sound is meant to accompany the visual medium and is not adequate for the task, then the entire enterprise fails. The most obvious connection to sound for the discipline is found in ethnomusicology and leading figures such as Steven Feld have demonstrated the power of sound in anthropological practice. As a linguist, ethnomusicologist, and anthropologist, Feld has made a profound impact both in the discipline and beyond noted in many interdisciplinary venues. His work in the later 20th century in Papua New Guinea foregrounded song and sound as primary focuses of his fieldwork which then translated to his outputs. His notion of schizophonic mimesis theorizes how sound can be removed from its primary context and rearranged and recognized differently as a separate context entirely (Feld 1996). This speaks to and influences the notion of "remixing" that not only defines popular music forms in the later 20th century, but is utilized as a notion in multimodal anthropology to discuss how work can be rearranged and recontexualized through collaborative work. Steven Feld's own capacities as a musician undoubtedly influenced his thinking as a pioneer in this aspect of the field. But what is he called? Is he ever labeled as an aural anthropologist or as a sound anthropologist in the same capacity someone working with film would possibly be labeled as a visual anthropologist?

In many ways, despite the prominence of Feld in the field, he suffers the same issue of marginalization as others who attempt modes of multimodal practice. Sound, in this case, is relegated to the same marginalization that early forms of visual work suffer. The film or photographic record is the evidence of "real" ethnographic work that occurs in fieldwork through note taking and various methodologies. Despite the albums and other sound platforms created by Feld and others, it still resides in the shadows of text as the primary mode of dissemination of anthropological knowledge. Work in ethnographic sound does not have a mode of dissemination except an emerging set of anthropologically focused anthropology podcasts. Digital audio platforms present a real possibility for centering this type of work. Yet, how does one publish sound? Maybe the cassette tape, vinyl album or 8-track tape? How is it supposed to be recognized as ethnographic work? The fieldwork interview taped on a variety of mediums must be transcribed, coded, and moved through the medium of text to be deemed meritorious. And, by the way, we highly encourage the reader to engage the ethnographic toadscapes of Steven Feld (Annan and Feld 2008: 134).

Yet, any fieldworker would attest to the importance of the aural in anthropological fieldwork. In a sensory approach to anthropology it stands as one of the primary five senses. One does not have to look far into the annals of the fields to find statements of "how the jungle sounded" for the lone anthropologist in the exotic field, or the decibel level of the "streetscape" for the urban anthropologist. Sound is there but it stands as evidence of *in situ* fieldwork and then must be described to the reader via text. Even when sound is the primary focus of ethnography, as in the work of Brian Larkin in Nigeria focusing on radio and colonialism, we do not hear the radio broadcasts nor the din of music and sound around the theaters that are his primary fieldsites (Larkin 2008). The work of pioneering ethnomusicologist Alan Lomax stands alone as a body of work that is recognized primarily for the actual sound that was created and recorded by him. But it is deemed scientific and relevant due to the context that surrounds it including his methodology and its housing in the Library of Congress. Anthropologists dedicated to ethnomusicology continue to push for the primacy of sound in anthropological fieldwork and outputs, as evidenced at the University of Sheffield. There have also been novel experiments with sound, video, and gallery installation as experienced through the project *Air Pressure* by Cox and Carlyle at the 2012 Ethnographic Terminalia (Carlyle and Cox 2012). We can even claim a basis for multimodality in classic cultural and media studies work. What can be said about Walter Benjamin, Marshall McLuhan, or John Berger that hasn't already been said? Plenty. Other anthropologists may have heard phrases such as the "medium is the message" or given it reference in the annals of the anthropology of media, but it has been given short shrift if any. Edward T. Hall was a very influential colleague of Marshall McLuhan and what is more multimodal than proxemics! John Berger's *Ways of Seeing* and the series produced on the BBC based on the book helped the public understand the dynamic between text, image, and culture in the interpretation of art. And, therefore, questioning the entire nature of art itself in its cultural and class context. That, in and of itself, is a very multimodal question.

Walter Benjamin's classic essay "Art in the age of mechanical production" has been utilized in many disciplines including anthropology where his canon is often added to known theorists in the discipline. Benjamin's premise that art loses an "aura" when reproduced has been utilized predominantly by our close cousins in cultural studies where most references to his work are the inevitable and necessary name drop. In any graduate seminar one must be ready to both pronounce his last name correctly and throw down on the impact of speed and reproduction of cultural material and the peril of losing meaning through the process. There have been wonderful visual interpretations of Benjamin's musings including the ethnographic film *In and Out of Africa* that reveals the transnational networks and valuation of "African art" (Pollack 1985). The parentheses are purposeful as the filmmaker shows how African masks and other objects are manufactured to look old to lend authenticity and value when traded on the open market, predominantly by West African art dealers. The secret to making a recently carved statue look hundreds of years old for the potential Western buyer? Shinola, chickens, chewed and spat out nuts and a good story that can be adapted in any commodity exchange on the Tony End of Long Island, New York.

Among many other somewhat rogue anthropologists discussed in the book, Paul Stoller is unique in anthropology in that he writes on multiple subjects, takes media seriously as a subject, has amazing insight into the lifeways of his collaborators, writes prolifically for both a public and academic audience, and he has been possessed in a ceremony conducting fieldwork. In the ethnography *Money Has No Smell: The Africanization of New York City*, Stoller provides a deeper glimpse into the transnational African art trade (Stoller 2002). He uses the tragic murder of unarmed Guinean street trader Amadou Diallo in 1999 as a touchstone for a discussion of West African immigrants. It is no accident that Paul Stoller gets his affinity for boundary crossing and experimentation from Jean Rouch (Stoller 1992). The iconic ethnographic filmmaker is seen as a progenitor for a multimodal anthropology where his media combined audio and video with performance and frivolity. We actually approach an assessment of multimodal work by asking WWJRD – what would Jean Rouch do? Even years after his death, Rouch stubbornly serves as a touchstone for evaluating ethnographic experimentation in practice, theory, and form.

His writings are limited but his musings are lengthy. The lore of his early work is nostalgic for any ethnographic filmmaker. In a series of essays that appear in *Anthropology of Visual Communication* one can see theory, method, auteurism, and critical interrogation emerge in his writing simultaneously with the films that he was making. Very few have been able to replicate this model and we champion the work of our colleague Harjant Gill as someone who has. It is the honesty that Rouch and Stoller bring to their work that also marks them as nascent multimodal iconoclasts. Whereas Malinowski plays an ethnographic shell game, Rouch revels in what is not supposed to be done and shows the crew, the food, the truck in the background, how he questions what he is doing, and even assuming different positionalities at times centering his compatriots as his co-authors. He consistently questions power dynamics, colonialism, and the way in which anthropological knowledge is portrayed and disseminated. Rouch's development of a "shared anthropology" is the grounding ethos for multimodal practices that are emergent today (Stoller 1989).

Obviously, anthropology is predominantly a text-based field that has utilized the visual as either illustrative of fieldwork practice or evidence of communities engaged in practice. It is all about the notes and the writing. While the visual was marginalized already, the emphasis on writing creates a turn that is so complete that those producing visual-based anthropological work are pressured to turn their work into a replication of writing with assessment hinging on whether media is ethnographic or not. The Society for Visual Anthropology has made significant efforts to validate visual media as academic work. Simultaneously, a large bulk of the writing around ethnographic film production and visual anthropology are attempts to justify this work as a form of ethnography that should be recognized in the discipline. This was never the question to begin with. Multimodal work that we see in visual anthropology was never meant to be a facsimile for written ethnography. As David MacDougall asserts, a different mode of epistemology exists in the visual. It creates a different way of knowing (MacDougall 2006). This expands even more when practice is centered on participatory and collaborative possibilities.

There was also an amazing time in anthropology when experimentation in multimodal forms was emerging, particularly through the Annenberg School. It is worth pausing to explore this prescient multimodal moment in anthropological thinking pulling on the zeitgeist of the times along with McLuhan, Berger, Eco, and others. Visual anthropology pioneer Sol Worth, who advocated, rather, for an anthropology of visual communication, experimented with participatory methodologies for media making with the project "Through Navajo eyes" which is seen as one of the first attempts to hand the camera to those who had always been in front of it (Worth et al. 1997). While steeped in some romanticism and colonial thinking, Worth was thinking critically about the "truthfulness" of what the camera could produce and the problematic power dynamics of working with indigenous populations in the United States. The project opened up perceptual ideas about creating an "ethnographic semiotic" and the idea of the possibilities of a "bio-documentary" to reframe communication to ascertain the "native" perception of the world. Reframed from the vantage of the 21st century this is somewhat naive and innocent but as Larry Gross states, Worth's work was beginning to open up an analytical shift prior to his untimely death in 1977:

> Worth was beginning to formulate two related sets of questions which he pursued for the rest of his life. First, he was led to tackle the question of how meaning can be communicated in various modes and media: are visual images in general, and film in particular, better. Understood in light of an overall theory of communication as symbolic behavior; and what would this theory look like? Second, he understood that his experience with novice filmmakers suggested a radical innovation in the way the film medium could be used as a research tool. If anyone could be taught to make a film that reflected his or her own world view, and the values and concerns of his or her group, then the direction of the film communication process could be reversed.
> (Gross 1980: 3)

In "Toward an ethnographic semiotic" Worth stresses the need for visual anthropologists to develop theories of interpreting film through the lens of semiotics. Worth contends that despite the historical usage of film in ethnography to attempt to create objective documents which record culture "truthfully," film must be recognized as symbolic "statements" which are laden with specific intentions, limitations, rules, and positionalities. In other words, the context in which media is created becomes primary in analysis. While not incredibly radical, his thinking nonetheless drew admirers ranging from Margaret Mead to Umberto Eco who upon Worth's death stated in a letter to Larry Gross that "Pictures can't say ain't but we can continue to say that Sol is through the ideas he gave us" (Umberto Eco, letter to Larry Gross 1980). And, in his "autobiographical obituary" published in 1977, Margaret Mead praises his unique contribution to the field:

> Originally an artist, he brought a new dimension to the facets ·of ethnographic filmmaking: a way in which people could document the world as they, themselves, saw it. Before the camera was put in the hands of those people who had previously been the subject of the anthropologist's investigation, we did not have an appropriate way of presenting their visual view of the world.
>
> (Gross 1980)

The "Through Navajo Eyes" project begat Terence "Terry" Turner's "Kayapo Video Project," Vincent Carelli's "Video in the Village" work, and the serious evaluation of indigenous media creation as a source for ethnographic speculation by anthropologists led by Faye Ginsburg. As a pillar in the visual anthropology universe, Ginsburg went on to claim indigenous produced film and video "as new vehicles for internal and external communication, for self-determination, and for resistance to outside cultural domination" (Ginsburg 1991: 92). This positioning of the authoritative indigenous voice is prescient in the centering of collaboration as a principle of multimodal anthropology.

There was also a strong emphasis on visual media and culture that emerged from Margaret Mead and her advocacy for visual anthropology. This coincides with the rise of the Annenberg School and individuals associated with the anthropology of visual communication. Other compatriots of Sol Worth hanging around included Ray Birdwhistell, Erving Goffman, Larry Gross, Dell Hymes, and Jay Ruby. Each contributed to an emphasis on the context of visual communication from the development of kinesics (Birdwhistell) and the emphasis on speech communities (Hymes) as primary sources for ethnographic analysis. Birdwhistell was part of the interdisciplinary Macy Conferences with Bateson, Mead, and others. The journal *Studies in Visual Communication* is a repository for what we would claim as a prominent multimodal moment. Edited by Larry Gross and Dell Hymes, the annals of the journal are replete with projects that would well fit a contemporary multimodal anthropology. From Rouch's early war stories of shared anthropology to musings on the legendary project *Chronicle of a Summer*. Other experimental contributions include an analysis of dance (Zarrilli 1983), a "sociovidistic" approach to children's filmmaking (Chalfen 1981), a proto-photovoice project in East Baltimore (Rich et al. 1981), cartography and power (Mukerji 1984), and graphics and demography (Watkins 1985), to name just a few.

24 *Multimodality*

These projects were unsteadily part of foundational visual anthropology works, but they never felt like visual anthropology *per se*. This is especially true as visual anthropology became a synonym for ethnographic film. Yet, even in this period journals such as *Visual Anthropology Review* under the stewardship of Lucien Taylor were featuring works that fit more comfortably under the rubric of an anthropology of visual communication or multimodal anthropology. Taylor's curated essays from 1990–1994 in *Visualizing Theory* were intended to "clear a space for the theoretical analysis of the ocular… and the analytic potential of visual media themselves, and thus try to further our understanding of modes of (non-linguistic) visual analysis" (Taylor 1994: xii). The structure of the book itself is divided between essay sections such as the ethnographic as ipsographic; surrealism, vision, and cultural criticism; the scopic and the haptic; and visualizing theory. The emphasis on self-recording and the merits of valuing collaborators weaved throughout these collected essays work as a pillar for a contemporary multimodal practice.

Contemporary Multimodality

It should not come as a surprise that the University of Pennsylvania has continued to be a space where experimentation in media and multimodal work continue the legacy of those who forged an anthropology of visual communication. For over a decade Deborah Thomas and John Jackson have been the spiritual leaders of a multimodal approach in the discipline and have guided a cohort of graduate students who are now professionals in the field and forging a multimodal approach. CAMRA (Collective for Advancing Multimodal Research Arts) has become a space for novel multimodal projects, writings, and convening of artists, anthropologists, and the broader community. CAMRA follows a mission to foster "interdisciplinary collaborations amongst scholars, sensory ethnographers, artists and educators within and beyond the University of Pennsylvania to explore, practice, evaluate and teach about multimedia research and representation" (www.camrapenn.org). This mission and the approach of CAMRA are to create guidelines for multimodal research, create spaces for multimodal work to be produced, and explore how technologies can affect pedagogy. The strong emphasis on participatory methodologies is a crucial part of the various projects that have emerged from CAMRA and, in turn, have influenced our emphasis on collaboration being the most important aspect of a multimodal practice.

When Deborah Thomas took over the editorship of *American Anthropologist*, her work with CAMRA drove the rebranding of the visual anthropology section of the journal to multimodal anthropologies. While there has been some hand wringing over this shift as noted, many have seen this as a move that opens up wider interpretations of work as multimodal, musings on what a multimodal approach entails and how to center experimental work as meritorious of inclusion in the journal. As the first editors of this newly branded section along with our colleague Harjant Gill, we took this charge from Deborah Thomas seriously and pushed to bring in novel forms of emerging multimodal work. As much of this chapter has detailed, our editorship and individual work has also led us to think critically about the pitfalls of multimodal work and a reclamation of what we see as nascent multimodal forms in anthropological history.

Simultaneously, colleagues in Europe have been striving toward shaping a multimodal approach and situating this work in the discipline. As noted, a recent venue for multimodal work is the journal *Multimodality and Society*. In the initial publication of the journal, long-time multimodal thinker Carey Jewitt and others called for contributions and research that show "a commitment to socially-orientated multimodal work that critically engages with contemporary challenges of multimodality, and advances the field of multimodality theoretically, methodologically or empirically" (Jewitt et al. 2021: 5). In doing so, the editorial board seeks to expand the "modes" of multimodality by going beyond multimodal work as a "visual-plus" approach. Rather, the focus of what the journal would like to feature focuses on "multimodal interactions" and "texts in action." And, much like other emerging multimodal practitioners, they hope to create a critical investigation of multimodality and deepen theoretical and methodological thinking for a multimodal approach.

Thus far the journal has featured a number of novel submissions that create a mixed bag of multimodal examples and speculations. Examples include Welcome and Thomas who bring questions of abstraction, witnessing, and refusal within their own media practices addressing violence in the Caribbean. They utilize these ideas to analyze how "something that feels like sovereignty circulates and is transmitted from one to another" (Welcome and Thomas 2021: 391) Khot et al. pursue a human-computer interaction approach to multimodality in the creation of a "human food interaction" project during the COVID pandemic entitled "Guardian of the snacks" described as "a tangible multimodal system that encourages mindful snacking by offering a playful companionship to snacking" (Khot et al. 2021: 153) The authors theorize solitary eating practices while also including schematics on the actual design of the apparatus used. Described as "naive" and without agency, "Guardian of the snacks" is a troublemaker and not a problem solver. It is a project that centers the actual process of designing an apparatus as much as addressing the cultural and physiological context of snacking. These and other contributions highlight elements of multimodal practice that center on collaboration, playfulness, and design. There is an attentiveness to the "broader landscape of interaction and communication" and, no doubt, the structural conditions in which that landscape is embedded leading to speculations of a "feminist multimodality" (Gupta 2021) and the "capitalist erotics in hip hop" (Maxwell and Greenaway 2022).

Figure 1.1 "Guardian of the snacks"
Source: Khot et al. (2021)

There have been a number of practitioners who have fully embraced a multimodal approach in their work. Many of our European colleagues have been resolutely multimodal as embodied in the work of Paolo S.H. Favero and the multimodal projects he has produced including apps, photography, and other experimental approaches. A self-described visual anthropologist with an interest in the role of images in human life, it is his interest and work in emerging technologies, politics, sensory ethnography, arts-based methodologies, and existentialism that places him as a leading exemplar of multimodal practice. There are numerous others that we would place in a rogue's gallery of multimodal practice including Elizabeth Chin whose various projects are part performative, design-based, and made as much for the gallery as ethnographic practice in Haiti. Her Laboratory of Speculative Ethnography centers the speculative nature of design "as a way to imagine objects freed from constraints of time, technological limitations, and other aspects of present reality" (Chin, n.d.). In addition to this work she has placed the choreography of Katherine Dunham as rooted in anthropological fieldwork and developed "African GoPros" to re-center the gendered use of this technology. She asks the pointed question, "What if GoPro accessories were engaged with African aesthetics and fashion?" And, while joyful, this question leads to a speculation on the utility of such objects interwoven into design to address and possibly record violence inflicted upon Black men. What is so crucial about Chin's multimodal work is that it does not shy away from levity, but brings a sense of humor into profound cultural questions. Her work centers process and the possibilities of local-based design.

Multimodality 27

Figure 1.2 Why should white guys and their dogs have all the fun? An Afro GoPro designed by Elizabeth Chin
Source: https://elizabethjchin.com/portfolio/afrogopros

Perhaps no other group has marked an emerging multimodal process more than the collective behind Ethnographic Terminalia. Over a decade-plus tenure this annual event linked to the American Anthropological Association Annual Meetings centers design and a variety of media in a gallery setting of experimental ethnographic practice and pushes the theoretical boundaries of curation, production, and exhibition. As both curators and anthropologists, this collective has made great strides toward continuing to legitimate what some may call alternative modes of scholarly production. Another way to describe this would be that they are forwarding a new multimodal anthropology and the field is catching up to it. Although some may argue that the tremendous and obvious amount of work that goes into Ethnographic Terminalia is outside the normal confines of scholarship, we have personally witnessed the impact this annual exhibit has made on colleagues and how much it pushes notions of multimodal work in anthropology. No less than Paul Stoller, in a review of the seventh Ethnographic Terminalia exhibit, noted that the collective "invites us to glimpse into the future and provides a much-appreciated tonic for our discipline" (Stoller 2015). The ability of the collective to translate multimodal work into a publicly engaged practice with an applied edge makes it truly unique. These "curatorial tactics" and practices open up critical spaces for participation, speculation, and collaborative possibilities. And, just like Elizabeth Chin, open up a space for joy in practice.

Another recent multimodal experiment with photography is *Writing with Light*, the dual project of the Society for Visual Anthropology and Society for Cultural Anthropology. This experiment in rejuvenating or, better yet, re-imagining the photo-essay uses the etymology of the word photograph as a premise for work. Using the standard photo-essay as a launching point, the collective hopes to create/rethink/utilize photography as a means for new epistemological ideas in anthropology. As they state:

> Writing with Light is an initiative to bolster the place of the photo-essay – and, by extension, formal experimentation – within international anthropological scholarship. As a collaboration between two journals published by the American Anthropological Association (AAA), *Cultural Anthropology* and *Visual Anthropology Review*, Writing with Light is led by a curatorial collective that aims to address urgent and important concerns about the sustained prominence of multimodal scholarship. Anthropological projects based in video, installation, performance, etc. take as a given that multimodality changes what anthropologists can and should see as productive knowledge.
> (Choi et al. 2019)

This notion of questioning both the visual as form and the typical *modus operandi* of publication venues and their standing in the discipline is at the heart of a multimodal approach that seeks to disrupt both the notion of authorship and who can fulfill that role. This is far beyond the standard use of photography in ethnographic monographs which usually serves as *in situ* proof of the fieldwork experience, or perhaps as a *tromp l'oeil* of an imagined ethnographic engagement. The deceptive quality of photography as proof of endeavor finds its roots in semiotics theory, art, and other fields. From asking the questions of "This is not a Pipe" to "Pictures can't say aint," the empirical authority of photography or artistic rendering should never be relied upon completely in its static form alongside text. This is what makes social media so interesting as a possible multimodal anthropological form. While typically utilized for its social and fun qualities by anthropologists at large, many such as Dick Powis are utilizing spaces such as Instagram as a fieldwork tool in terms of its research and connectivity, possibilities to collaborators, and as a means of illustrating fieldwork and eliciting comments. This is the argument we were trying to make in *Networked Anthropology* in 2014. Social media should not be seen as a leisurely activity outside of the scope of anthropological inquiry much like television was decades ago, but as a multimodal space that creates novel networks and collaborative capacities with our collaborators where the idea of authorship begins to crumble.

Conclusion

We attempt to define multimodal anthropology as an approach that is:

> both descriptive and prescriptive. It characterizes the way people work and conduct research in the contemporary world, and implores us to conceive of anthropological research and scholarship beyond the finished, reified products of fieldwork or labwork: an article, a book, an ethnographic film, a photo essay. Instead, we are encouraged to engage in varying processes of knowledge production that often lead to multiple outcomes. Prescriptively, multimodal anthropology asks that we take these outcomes and processes seriously as meaningful interventions that nudge anthropology into more collaborative, innovative, and reflexive directions.
>
> (Collins et al. 2017: 1)

With this guiding ethos in place, we sought to recruit work and perspectives from colleagues who we saw already operating in the multimodal space. This resulted in welcomed extensions by Elizabeth Chin and Dick Powis who we feature in this chapter as exemplars of multimodal anthropology. For Chin, a multimodal anthropology opens up a number of possibilities to broaden methods, make work in new ways, and challenge what counts as knowledge production. As an anthropologist in a design school, she also challenges anthropologists to bring elements of design such as form, process, and materials into their work and calls for a possible "participant making" as a form of collaboration that leads to an "iterative process of manifesting ideas as thing" (Chin 2017: 543). For Dick Powis, who was in graduate school at the time we requested an essay from him, he sees the collaborative possibilities of a multimodal approach to invite his Senagelese colleagues into his ethnographic process:

> For me, multimodality means publicly documenting the trajectory of my research through text, images, and video across blogs and social media platforms like Instagram, Twitter, and Facebook. My goal is not only to report the data in near real time but also to demonstrate to my audience the process of what I do as an ethnographer. My hope is that I can successfully invite both my academic audiences and colleagues in the United States and my interlocutors in Senegal to engage with me and with each other in dialogue about the research topic and the research design.
>
> (Powis 2017: 361)

Despite the engagement and collaborative nature that this methodology opens up for his research, Powis expresses his frustration that a multimodal approach is met with skepticism from senior colleagues who see it as "extracurricular" and possibly even ethically problematic. These same tensions have faced the inclusion of visual anthropology in the discipline for years. What these senior colleagues miss is that an engagement of multimodality does not mean that one drops the hallmarks of ethnographic research but expands them further into participatory and collaborative modes. And, perhaps, even working to decolonize the field. Thus, one has to ask, why the resistance? It may be technophobia, but it also reveals a tension and fear of letting go of authorial superiority and exclusiveness which feed the worst parts of the discipline historically and contemporaneously.

Ironically, many folks who kept various technologies such as social media at arm's length in their work and ethnographic speculation suddenly emerged as "digital anthropologists" when the COVID-19 pandemic emerged globally in 2020. With the loss of the physical field, anthropologists began to question if they could simply move into the digital field. The assumption that you can just move your fieldwork to a digital space operates on the premise that with the absence of the anthropologist in the physical field that the community all of a sudden becomes static or disappears. But guess what, social and cultural life continues and people document and comment on things in their own communities and do not need a Zoom platform and anthropologist in the mix to do so. This forces an uncomfortable question we posed during the pandemic of whether or not "the field" actually needs anthropologists at all and the imbrication of anthropology in the processes of advanced capitalism, i.e. travel to "exotic" places and a reliance on corporeal presence enshrined from Malinowski onward. It is well known that digital technologies that became necessary during the pandemic further exposed multiple digital divides and emboldened the conceit that digital anthropology would provide a "workaround" to presence in the field. As we noted at the time, "we are all used to that peculiar hypocrisy in anthropology that decries colonization and its authorizing gaze, but that still seems to insist on presence in order to undertake anthropology. Perhaps enough of that" (Collins and Durington 2020)?

Similarly, Proctor sardonically questioned newly emergent digital anthropologists at the time as well, "So you want to 'do' digital ethnography?" Proctor provides some pointers for work while simultaneously warning fledgling digital anthropologists forced into virtual spaces because of the so-called loss of the field that "Lurking is a great practice for preparatory research, but it is a poor ethnographic methodology" (Proctor 2020). The truism here is that one does not do covert anthropology and in these virtual spaces one must make themselves visible through presence and actions. This may seem contradictory to a multimodal anthropology that questions the ethnographic authority of *in situ* fieldwork. Not quite. A multimodal anthropology seeks to complicate and open up notions of presence with a conscious attentiveness to shifting authority, who produces ethnographic knowledge, and consistent presence through collaboration in myriad spaces. What multimodal anthropology asserts is, simply, that the field doesn't really need us to exist. And, with that acknowledgment and questioning of presence, new possibilities begin to emerge.

Dattatreyan and Marrero-Guillamón call for an "inventive" anthropology through a multimodal approach that opens up pedagogical possibilities and looks, just as we do, to Rouch and others for inspiration (Dattatreyan and Marrero-Guillamón 2019). Following this strain of inventive strides, Shankar has advocated "listening to images" through pedagogical interactions posing questions in analysis to images such as "What do you see? What do you hear? What does it want?" (Shankar 2019: 229). Other projects that became part of the nascent multimodal anthropologies section in *American Anthropologist* explore postcards (Gugganig and Schor 2020), theater (Vidali 2020), performance (Cool 2020), drawing (Hurdley et al. 2017), remixing music (Bitter 2023), and smartphones (Favero and Theunissen 2018). Simultaneously, Chio argues as well that we have yet to determine a means of reviewing multimodal work and this must be developed not only for the discipline but for the public as well (Chio 2017), while Takaragawa and her co-authors warn of "Bad Habitus" and that there is nothing particularly "liberatory" in multimodal work if it is imbricated in global capitalism (Takaragawa et al. 2019).

Other multimodal extensions have emerged in recent years. Upon the completion of our term as editors of the inaugural multimodal section we were incredibly pleased (as most editors are) to hand off the section to our colleagues who represent a generation after us and have emerged from a period in anthropology and society in general where multimodality is akin to common sense. After all, we had dial up modems in college and they never had to listen to that sonic cacophany. Whereas we were fielding, if not begging, for contributions from the field, we had the hope that the trend lines were pointing in the direction of more robust contributions and the welcomed complications that come with them continuing to question the notion and possible contribution a multimodal anthropology could make to the field. Patracia Astacio, Gabriel Dattatreyan, and Arjun Shankar continue to curate and explore multimodal directions but also signal a "multimodal ambivalence in sh*t times" warning that we must remain vigilant lest we fall into technological determinism and avoid uncritical engagements with digital communications technologies (Astacio et al. 2021). Written as a manifesto, they rightly ground this ambivalence in the danger of the illusion of democratic notions of technology. And we have been incredibly encouraged by the activities and writings from former members of Ethnographic Terminalia.

In our exit essay as editors we asserted that multimodal anthropology has the promise "to reveal the limits of anthropological work, to critique its embeddedness in power and inequality, and to gesture to forms of practice that may be more inclusive, more emancipatory, and, ultimately, more hopeful for a better world for our interlocutor and for ourselves" (Collins et al. 2021: 193). We continue to be hopeful and encouraged, but as our colleagues warn, simultaneously remain vigilant and somewhat ambivalent as well. There is a lot of very cool work out there and emerging in the field.

32 Multimodality

Example: Anatomy of a Multimodal Project

What does multimodal anthropology look like? In many ways, this is an odd question to ask, since the whole point of "multimodal" is the engagement with a variety of media platforms. Even so, there are some characteristics that all forms of multimodal anthropology have in common.

Figure 1.3 shows a walking tour we did with community groups in South Baltimore in 2016, one that sought to highlight both the historical importance of this Black neighborhood and the various threats to the community from encroaching gentrification. Is this the very best example of multimodality? Perhaps not – but it is in some ways representative, as defined by these chief characteristics:

1. Multimedia: This tour combines text, photographs, recordings, and geolocation, along with links to videos of ethnographic interviews, websites, and online news articles.
2. Accessible: When we began to plan for this research, we looked at a variety of platforms that might support this tour (including print). Ultimately, we decided on this site, a commercial platform developed originally for museum tours. Our thinking was that the tour would be available both on the website (as per the screenshot) and on the mobile app, and that this would, ultimately, be more accessible to more people in more ways than a strictly print publication.

Figure 1.3 A screenshot of the izi.travel walking tour of Sharp Leadenhall
Source: https://izi.travel/en/d7d2-sharp-leadenhall-walking-tour/en

Multimodality 33

3   Collaborative: This project was the result of multiple collaborations. First, it represents a long-term collaboration with Ms. Betty Bland Thomas, a neighborhood activist and President of the South Baltimore Partnership, along with other community groups in Sharp Leadenhall, including churches and other residents. Secondly, this was a collaboration with Baltimore City youth interning at a non-profit in Baltimore, Wide Angle Youth Media. These media producers worked with us to edit the audio. Finally, this was a collaboration with our students, who we sent (as extra credit) on the tour, collecting along the way their thoughts and comments.

4   Interactive: When you go on the tour, you begin at the sign for the neighborhood ("Welcome to the Sharp Leadenhall Historic Community"), and proceed along the stops from 1 to 21. When users get close to the next site, the geolocated content begins in the form of an audio recording. For the tour to work, then, you need to move through the tour, a form of interactivity that combines what Michel de Certeau called the "long poem of walking" with the more descriptive goals of ethnographic research. (de Certeau 1984: 101).

5   Ethical: As we will describe in the following chapter, this project is "ethical" in at least two ways. First, the work was done alongside communities in ways that were important to the community. This walking tour, for example, was made to help underscore the historical importance of the neighborhood as a Black community. In this sense, it represents a more recent movement in anthropology away from "knowledge for its own sake" to a situated knowledge that seeks to contribute to the communities in which we work. Yet, the tour is "ethical" in another way: it prompts ethical reflection and discussion.

Classroom Exercise

What kinds of media are salient in the lives of your students? What do they consume? What do they create? And how do those acts of consumption and creation connect them, to other people and to communities? One of our insights into multimodal anthropology is that people, in their capacities of both interpretive communities of media and as content creators, are astute students of their own communities, and that their work may overlap with anthropology in ways that need to be recognized and honored.

This activity could include several parts:

1   Journaling. Students should document and describe their own *Media Worlds* (Ginsburg et al. 2002). These can include the mass media, of course, but any media should also be considered – from text to comics to social media.

2   Discussion. Students should compare insights into their media worlds with each other, concentrating on the activities and platforms they have

in common. Discussion should include notes on the practice of media. How do students make and post a video? How do they edit photos? Decide on captions? How do people interpret the media around them? And where? If there's a platform (e.g., Discord), what are the rules for that community?

References

Annan, N.O., & Feld, S. (2008). *Bufo variations*. VoxLox.

Astacio, P.A., Dattatreyan, E.G., & Shankar, A. (2021). Multimodal ambivalence. *American Anthropologist*, 123(2), 420–430.

Bitter, J. (2023). Sampling as ethnographic method/remixing Gulu City. *American Anthropologist*, 125, 23–35. https://doi.org/10.1111/aman.13804.

Brown, A., Coote, J., & Gosden, C. (2000). Tylor's tongue. *Journal of the Anthropological Society of Oxford*, 31(3), 257–276.

Caffrey, M., & Francis, P. (2009). *To cherish the life of the world: The selected letters of Margaret Mead*. Basic Books.

Carlyle, A., & Cox, R. (2012). *Air pressure* [CD and book]. Gruenrekorder.

Cerwonka, A., & Malkki, L.H. (2008). *Improvising theory: Process and temporality in ethnographic fieldwork*. University of Chicago Press.

Chalfen, R. (1981). A sociovidistic approach to children's filmmaking: The Philadelphia project. *Studies in Visual Communication*, 7(1), 2–32. https://repository.upenn.edu/svc/vol7/iss1/2.

Chin, E. (2017). Lab of speculative anthropology. https://elizabethjchin.com/portfolio/afrogopros/.

Chio, J. (2017). Guiding lines. *Cultural Anthropology*, May 2. https://culanth.org/fieldsights/1118-guiding-lines.

Choi, V., Westmoreland, M., Shankar, A., Campbell, C., & Douglas, L. (2019). Final writing with light series. *Cultural Anthropology*, October 29. https://culanth.org/fieldsights/series/final-writing-with-light-series.

Collins, S.G. (2008). *All tomorrow's cultures: Anthropological engagements with the future* (new edn). Berghahn Books. www.jstor.org/stable/j.ctt9qdc78.

Collins, S.G., & Durington, M. (2014). *Networked anthropology: A primer for ethnographers*. Routledge.

Collins, S.G., & Durington, M.S. (2020). The case for letting anthropology be quarantines: COVID and the end of ethnographic presence. *Entanglements*, 3(2), 92–96.

Collins, S.G., Durington, M., & Gill, H. (2017). Multimodality: An invitation. *American Anthropologist*, 119, 142–146. https://doi.org/10.1111/aman.12826.

Collins, S., Durington, M., & Gill, H. (2021). The uncertain present and the multimodal future. *American Anthropologist*, 123, 191–193. https://doi.org/10.1111/aman.13535.

Cool, J. (2020). Tripod: Performance, media, cybernetics. *American Anthropologist*, 122, 684–690. https://doi.org/10.1111/aman.13436.

Dattatreyan, E.G. (2015). Social media-inspired self-portraits. *Visual Anthropology Review*, 31, 134–146. https://doi.org/10.1111/var.12077.

Dattatreyan, E.G., & Marrero-Guillamón, I. (2019). Introduction: Multimodal anthropology and the politics of invention. *American Anthropologist*, 121, 220–228. https://doi.org/10.1111/aman.13183.

De Certeau, M. (1984). *The practice of everyday life*. California University Press.
Favero, P.S.H., & Theunissen, E. (2018). With the smartphone as field assistant: Designing, making, and testing EthnoAlly, a multimodal tool for conducting serendipitous ethnography in a multisensory world. *American Anthropologist*, 120, 163–167. https://doi.org/10.1111/aman.12999.
Feld, S. (1996). Pygmy POP. A genealogy of schizophonic mimesis. *Yearbook for Traditional Music*, 28, 1–35. https://doi.org/10.2307/767805.
Ginsburg, F. (1991). Indigenous media: Faustian contract or global village? *Cultural Anthropology*, 6(1), 92–112.
Ginsburg, F.D., Abu-Lughod, L., & Larkin, B. (2002). *Media worlds: Anthropology on new terrain*. University of California Press.
Gross, L. (1980). Sol Worth and the study of visual communications. *Studies in Visual Communication*, 6(3), 2–19. https://repository.upenn.edu/svc/vol6/iss3/2.
Gugganig, M., & Schor, S. (2020). Multimodal ethnography in/of/as postcards. *American Anthropologist*, 122, 691–697. https://doi.org/10.1111/aman.13435.
Gupta, H. (2021). Feminist multimodality: A retrospective account of an exhibition on speculative urbanism. *Multimodality & Society*, 1(3), 281–299. https://doi.org/10.1177/26349795211027693.
Hakken, D. with Andrews, B. (1993). Book reviews: *Computing myths, class realities: An ethnography of technology and working people in Sheffield, England*. David Hakken with Barbara Andrews.. *Social Science Computer Review*, 14(2), 241–242. https://doi.org/10.1177/089443939601400218.
Hurdley, R., Biddulph, M., Backhaus, V., Hipwood, T., & Hossain, R. (2017). Drawing as radical multimodality: Salvaging Patrick Geddes's material methodology. *American Anthropologist*, 119, 748–753. https://doi-org.proxy-tu.researchp ort.umd.edu/10.1111/aman.12963
Jewitt, C., Adami, E., Archer, A., Björkvall, A., & Lim, F.V. (2021). Editorial. *Multimodality & Society*, 1(1), 3–7. https://doi.org/10.1177/2634979521992902.
Jobson, R.C. (2020). The case for letting anthropology burn. *American Anthropologist*, 122(2), 259–271.
Khot, R.A., Aggarwal, D., Yi, J.-Y. (Lois), & Prohasky, D. (2021). Guardian of the snacks: Toward designing a companion for mindful snacking. *Multimodality & Society*, 1(2), 153–173. https://doi.org/10.1177/26349795211007092.
Larkin, B. (2008). *Signal and noise: Media, infrastructure, and urban culture in Nigeria*. Duke University Press. https://doi.org/10.2307/j.ctv1220mnp.
MacDougall, D. (2006). *The corporeal image: Film, ethnography, and the senses* (student edn). Princeton University Press. www.jstor.org/stable/j.ctt4cgb17.
Marcus, G., & Fischer, M. (1986). *Anthropology as cultural critique: An experimental moment in the history of social sciences*. University of Chicago Press.
Markham, A.N. (2012). Fabrication as ethical practice: Qualitative inquiry in ambiguous internet contexts. *Information, Communication & Society*, 15, 334–353.
Maxwell, K., & Greenaway, J. (2022). Understanding "flow": A multimodal reading of political economy and capitalist erotics in hip hop. *Multimodality & Society*, 2 (4), 410–433. https://doi.org/10.1177/26349795221136859.
Mukerji, C. (1984). Visual language in science and the exercise of power: The case of cartography in early modern Europe. *Studies in Visual Communication*, 10(3), 30–45. https://repository.upenn.edu/svc/vol10/iss3/4.
Nerner, D. (2022). *Technologies of the oppressed*. The MIT Press.

Petch, A. (2006). Counting and calculating: Some reflections on using statistics to examine the history and shape of the collections at the Pitt Rivers Museum. *Journal of Museum Ethnography*, 18, 149–156. www.jstor.org/stable/40793818.

Pollack, S. (1985). *Out of Africa*. Universal Pictures.

Powis, R. (2017). Heartened by iconoclasm: A few preliminary thoughts about multimodality. *American Anthropologist*, 119(2), 359–361. https://10.1111/aman.12870.

Proctor, D. (2020). So you want to "do" digital ethnography?https://thegeekanthropologist.com/2020/03/25/so-you-want-to-do-digital-ethnography/.

Rich, L.G., Netherwood, J.C., & Cahn, E.B. (1981). East Baltimore: Tradition and transition. A documentary photography project (photo essay). *Studies in Visual Communication*, 7(3), 58–75. https://repository.upenn.edu/svc/vol7/iss3/4.

Saka, E. (2008). Blogging as a research tool for ethnographic fieldwork. ASA Media Anthropology Network, e-seminar series. https://johnpostill.wordpress.com/2008/05/14/blogging-as-a-research-tool-for-ethnographic-fieldwork/.

Shankar, A. (2019). Listening to images, participatory pedagogy, and anthropological (re-)inventions. *American Anthropologist*, 121, 229–242. https://doi.org/10.1111/aman.13205.

Sontag, S. (1966). *Against interpretation, and other essays*. Farrar, Straus & Giroux.

Stocking, G.W. (1984). From Rousseau to Rivers. *RAIN*, 61, 6–8.

Stoller, P. (1989). *The taste of ethnographic things: The senses in anthropology*. University of Pennsylvania Press. www.jstor.org/stable/j.ctt3fhjx9.

Stoller, P. (1992). *The cinematic Griot: The ethnography of Jean Rouch*. University of Chicago Press.

Stoller, P. (2002). *Money has no smell: The Africanization of New York City*. University of Chicago Press. https://doi.org/10.7208/9780226775265.

Stoller, P. (2015). The bureau of memories: Archives and ephemera. *Fieldsights*, March 20. https://culanth.org/fieldsights/the-bureau-of-memories-archives-and-ephemera.

Sunderland, P.L. (1999). Fieldwork and the phone. *Anthropological Quarterly*, 72(3), 105–117.

Takaragawa, S., Smith, T.L., Hennessy, K., Alvarez Astacio, P., Chio, J., Nye, C., & Shankar, S. (2019). Bad habitus: Anthropology in the age of the multimodal. *American Anthropologist*, 121, 517–524. https://doi.org/10.1111/aman.13265.

Taylor, L. (1994). *Visualizing theory: Selected essays from V.A.R. 1990–1994*. Routledge.

Vannini, P. (2019). *Doing public ethnography: How to create and disseminate ethnographic and qualitative research to a wide audience*. Routledge.

Vidali, D. (2020). Ethnographic theater making: Multimodal alchemy, knowledge, and invention. *American Anthropologist*, 122, 394–409. https://doi.org/10.1111/aman.13387.

Waltrop, K. (2017). Digital technologies, dreams and disconcertment in anthropological worldmaking. In J.F. Salazar, S. Pink, A. Irving, & J. Sjöberg (eds), *Anthropologies and futures*. Routledge, pp. 101–116.

Wang, A. (2012). Writing live fieldnotes: Towards a more open ethnography. *Ethnography Matters*. http://ethnographymatters.net/blog/2012/08/02/writing-live-fieldnotes-towards-a-more-open-ethnography/.

Watkins, S.C. (1985). Graphics in demography. *Studies in Visual Communication*, 11(3), 2–21. https://repository.upenn.edu/svc/vol11/iss3/2.

Welcome, L.A., & Thomas, D.A. (2021). Abstraction, witnessing, and repair; or, how multimodal research can destabilize the coloniality of the gaze. *Multimodality & Society*, 1(3), 391–406. https://doi.org/10.1177/26349795211042771.

Worth, S., Adair, J., & Chalfen, R. (1997). *Through Navajo eyes: An exploration in film communication and anthropology*. University of New Mexico Press.

Zarrilli, P. (1983). A microanalysis of performance structure and time in Kathakali dance-drama. *Studies in Visual Communication*, 9(3), 50–69. https://repository.upenn.edu/svc/vol9/iss3/5.

2 Old Questions and New Directions

This chapter will discuss common ethical concerns in anthropology and how networked media, collaboration, and other aspects of multimodal anthropology point the field in new directions by opening up new methods with communities. This means struggling to negotiate various "digital divides," but also new possibilities for overcoming obstacles to a truly collaborative anthropology. We also explain why we consider this work as formative of "sites" rather than simply the application of various "tools" – that the multimodal extends the fieldsite in interesting (and always problematic) ways. We will set up Chapters 3–7 where we will lay out how we have practiced multimodal anthropology.

If you are undertaking research (multimodal or otherwise), chances are good that you have filled out a variety of forms on "human subjects" for your IRB (Institutional Review Board). Some of these bureaucratic steps will most likely seem prudent. Certainly, when we work with student researchers, it makes perfect sense to have them go through a process that asks them to think about whom they're going to work with, what kinds of questions people will be asked, and what will happen to those data later. On the other hand, as many anthropologists have noted, the university IRB is largely premised on the production of research knowledge and the mitigation of risk at the level of the university (Annas 2006). Moreover, some of the most egregious research has had full IRB approval from host institutions, e.g., Johns Hopkins's Kennedy Krieger Institute and a study of lead paint abatement in the 1990s (Bozeman and Hirsch 2006). The ethical review process can, in other words, result in patently (even obviously) unethical research.

One of the problems with the IRB process (and there are many) stems from the nature of the human subjects review itself. It takes what (in anthropology) is a research project that unfolds in a broad context of history, politics, and power, and replaces it with an essentialized, dyadic encounter between "researcher" and "subject." In the case of the Johns Hopkins research (which was biomedical), the relevant contexts included structural racism, environmental "slow violence" in the form of lead paint, and an institutional history in which Johns Hopkins has exploited Baltimore's African American community as experimental subjects and as a

DOI: 10.4324/9781003330851-3

source of data (e.g., Henrietta Lacks). Ultimately, then, one could gain the approval of individual "subjects" without addressing this larger social and historical context. It may well be true, as Stuart Plattner notes, that, in his time as Program Director for the NSF, he "never learned of one case in which a respondent was actually harmed from participation in anthropological research," yet the ethics of anthropology must incorporate more than this level of "risk" (Plattner 2006: 526).

While direct harm may be something that is relatively rare in anthropology (although see Patrick Tierney 2001), it is clear that anthropology has a good deal of work to do with ethics in terms of these larger contexts. If we acknowledge the colonial history of the field, its complicity in subjugating the powerless, and its continued investment in technologies of "othering," there would seem to be an ethical obligation to not only face that history, but to intervene in its reproduction, even if that means, as Ryan Cecil Jobson has put it, "letting anthropology burn" (Jobson 2020). Certainly, the reckoning that has led to a call for an "abolitionist anthropology" has been a long time coming, and points to the difference between an "ethics" as a transactional accounting between "scientist" and "subject" and something more like justice (Shange 2022).

At the same time, with regard to relations, rapport, contexts, understandings, judgments, and comparisons, it would be hard to find a discipline more ethical in its orientation, even if, as Pels points out, the ethical orientations of the past are the exact opposite of ethical behavior today (Pels 1999). But more than this, the "codification" of anthropological ethics has led to the effacement of many of the powerful contexts that have historically shaped the field – from its embeddedness in eugenics and colonialism to its complicity with neoliberalism. As Pels (1999: 110) continues:

> The significance of this becomes apparent when we recapitulate what went before, in particular that the professionalization of anthropology was partly accomplished through the definition of a dyadic relationship between anthropologists and people studied, from which the colonial situation, its representations, and its values have been erased.

Paradoxically, the "ethical code" can look decidedly unethical, particularly in a discipline where context is everything. And at a time when anthropologists have called for the field to shift to an emphasis on anti-racism and decolonization and "eschew an exceptionalism that places itself outside these histories of violence," the technocratic fix of human subjects review and IRBs seems at best palliative, and at worst a screen behind which anthropology can continue down an exploitative path (Jobson 2020: 267). Research in anthropology can only constitute a "dyad" when everything else is suppressed – the histories, the power relationships, the webs of social life.

But wasn't ethics in anthropological work supposed to be more than a human subjects review anyway? As Caplan points out:

> the ethics of anthropology is clearly not just about obeying a set of guidelines; it actually goes to the heart of the discipline: the premises on which its practitioners operate, its epistemology, theory and praxis. In other words, what is anthropology for? Who is it for? Do its ethics need to be re-thought every generation, as the discipline's conditions of existence change?
>
> (Caplan 2003: 3)

If anthropology is about how we humans live, and is always already about how we should live, then the ethics of anthropology will be a continuous process, one that includes the reflection on the way one way of life is dependent on the subjugation of others and that responds to shifting forms of power. So, while there is no knowledge that is anterior to ethics, to practice anthropology is to undertake ethical inquiry. For all that, there are many examples of people and research that are clearly unethical, so there's no letting anthropology's colonial past (or present) off the hook, just as there is no excuse for unethical behavior by individual anthropologists today. But what this does do is center the field on ethical critique and reflection, one that demands that anthropologists examine the changing ethics of their field.

In this chapter, we turn to multimodal anthropology as an ethical inquiry. What do we mean by that? Not, of course, that there is anything inherently ethical about multimodal approaches. In fact, with its insistence on community collaboration, the multimodal anthropology we describe is fairly fraught with ethical quagmires. Nor do we mean that other subfields of anthropology are somehow "less" ethical. Merely that multimodality problematizes anthropology by foregrounding ethical dilemmas and ethical responsibilities that were certainly present in previous anthropological approaches, but were more submerged. We would caution against a technological determinism that imputes ethical problems to technologies themselves. Rather, the different "modalities" in the continuously unfolding "multimodal moment" of anthropology turn attention to questions that already existed. Our argument turns the usual human subjects / IRB concerns on their head. Multimodal anthropology is ethically important because it offers us opportunities for increased ethical engagement. In other words, multimodality pushes the ethical envelope, and demands that we examine these constellations of power and social relations with new eyes.

Shortly after the *American Anthropologist* debuted its "Multimodal Anthropology" section in 2017, Takaragawa et al. (2019: 517) published a critical essay that sounded a cautionary note:

> Multimodal anthropology – characterized for example by the use of sound, photography, video, art, drawings, digitally produced graphic

novels, performances, installation art, social media, cloud-based software, and mobile phones (and much more could and will be added to this list) – is a set of practices often deeply implicated in the digital and its invisible networks and resource-hungry requirements. If we are to take obligations within multimodal praxis seriously, we have to ask questions such as: how does the use of innovative technology elide and contribute to injustice and violences of extractive economies?

Actually, one could ask these questions of any medium. Even if, for example, we consider "installation art" outside of digital platforms where they may be disseminated, there are still questions. Who gets to make art? Who gets to exhibit? Who gets to challenge? Who funds it? What happens to the installation afterwards? Where is the actual gallery located in the racialized cartography of a particular city? All of the questions we might level at a digital platform are also relevant to any media that anthropologists might utilize in the production and communication of ethnographically intended work – including textuality. The ethnographic monograph – published in English, sold at a cost well above the monthly income of many of the world's peoples, archived in libraries that are inaccessible to those outside of the university system. How could this not be an example of the "violences of extractive economies"? And, if so, what makes multimodality any different? We are not even going to mention journal paywalls.

Multimodality, as we wrote in the first chapter, is not different. After all, what is multimodal today has its roots in the very beginnings of the anthropological project, and while, say, digital recording marks a significant departure from the analog past, it would be a mistake to miss the embeddedness of John Lomax's project in the very same regimes of exploitation that Takaragawa et al. critique (Cole 2018). Jean Rouch built bridges for a colonial power and then went back to blow them up after all. Nevertheless, a digitized recording embedded in social media networks controlled by corporations changes the calculus of that exploitation, from white constructions of African American folkways to Moby's sampling of Vera Hall in the 1980s to a website (whosampled.com) listing 14 tracks that have sampled Vera Hall's "Trouble So Hard" and hundreds of subreddits weighing in on samples of Hall's song being used in advertising. Plus, where does Moby even sit on the rankings of great sampling in music? We would undoubtedly rank it on the lower end of that list.

A digitized "Trouble So Hard" presents a different level of exploitation (and, perhaps, resistance) than "Trouble So Hard" as an analog recording. The difference lies in the sociotechnical system that includes capitalism, media, platforms, practice, and power relations. What changes as we move from one medium to another? To say that the digital introduces a decisive break would be a mistake: racism and cultural appropriation look much the same in 2023 as they did in 1930. But what has changed is that the sampled, networked recording highlights certain structures of power that may have been (implicitly) present before, but are now more clearly visible – like a n-dimensional polytope that seems to change shape in our three-dimensional world. We can represent this as a series of concentric circles extending out from a medium – in this case a photograph. In each of the four quadrants (technology, production, consumption, and network) of Figure 2.1, the photograph is embedded in a series of circles. Each quadrant, and each circle within the quadrant, adds another dimension of power and inequality.

Is the photo on Instagram different from the photo in an archive? Of course it is – even if the photo looks the same. Each quadrant is different, with different organizations of image production and consumption. The way the platform works is, of course, also relevant – the caption, the filtering, the tagging. Finally, the image is connected media and includes, in its network, followers, and people who found your post through other means (e.g., keywords, collabs, cross-posting, etc.). In turn, each of these levels yields ethical dilemmas regarding meaning, access, identity, politics, power. Yet to suggest that ethical dilemmas are somehow inherent to an Instagram photo ignores the ethical dilemmas inherent in all photography – which, whether in an archive, an exhibit, or a magazine, is likewise platform dependent. With a photo on social media, the networked dimensions rise to the fore, since it's not just about how many people see something, it's about the connections they have to each other (Collins and Durington 2014).

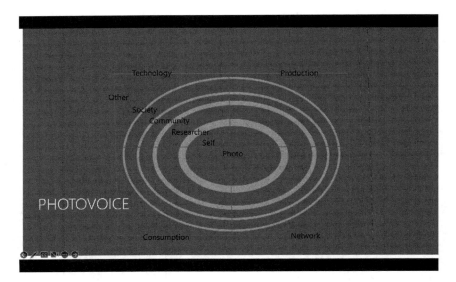

Figure 2.1 Concentric circles of power and inequality

Multimodal Ethics

What we have in mind is something like Astacio et al.'s "ambivalent multimodality":

> For us, an ambivalent multimodal anthropology "stays with the trouble" (Haraway 2016) and perhaps even makes trouble. Rather than pivoting on false binaries, an ambivalent multimodality recognizes and critiques the ways in which the digital (re)produces neocolonial forms of extraction, exclusion, inequality, and representational problematics. Yet, an ambivalent multimodality doesn't necessarily stay at the level of critique or recognition; it also seeks to open spaces of hope and speculative possibility; an ambivalent multimodality allows us to utilize the detritus of capitalist technoscience and encourages us to hack its latest advances to invent new pathways for share representation, all the while staying with the reflexive recognition of knowing that we are, in multiple ways, complicit.
> (Astacio et al. 2021: 421)

Those binarisms involve the utopian/dystopian dichotomies in which technologies are routinely slotted, a deterministic understanding that conceals a great deal of ideological work under cover of its materialist "objectivity." Accordingly, each example of multimodality brings with it an embeddedness in powerful systems of inequalities, and also suggests different avenues for resistance and for thinking "otherwise." Here, we discuss three, broad constellations of ethics and multimodality: collaboration, the digital divide, and the problem of ownership. Of course, there are many more ethical issues in multimodal anthropology, and many of these will be familiar to any anthropologist – e.g., an insistence on transparency, an ethical principle that has been an issue in anthropological ethics (however ambiguously) since Boas's 1919 letter to *The Nation* taking to task "a number of men who follow science as their profession, men whom I refuse to designate any longer as scientists, have prostituted science by using it as a cover for their activities as spies" (p. 1).

Collaboration

Just like the "informer" and "interlocutor," "collaborator" has a number of negative connotations. Working with an authoritarian regime, co-operating with the police, plotting with co-conspirators; all of these might earn you the title of "collaborator." As Chin (2016) notes, it "carries with it more than a whiff of betrayal." In the same "fieldsites" section, Shange recounts the series of co-optations and bad-faith appropriations at the school where she worked, as critical voices were twisted into support for the status quo:

I am hesitant to recount this incident; it reeks of collaborative treachery. The research collaboration between myself and the institution, the social-justice school's collaborative relationship with the community it serves, and its supposedly democratic governance structure are each thrown into crisis.

(Shange 2016)

As Shange suggests, "collaboration" in anthropology involves co-operation on a series of levels between different agents: self, institution, community. And along with these co-operations comes the possibility of bad faith, of betrayal, and of misunderstanding.

It is even unclear if all parties in a "collaboration" believe they are working on the same project. In his essay on Griaule's anthropology, James Clifford identifies two "modes" or "phases" in Griaule's work with the Dogon – a "documentary" and an "initiatory" phase. The "documentary" mode was marked by a struggle for colonial dominance:

Griaule assumed that the opposing interests of ethnographer and native could never be entirely harmonized. Relations sometimes romanticized by the term rapport were really negotiated settlements, outcomes of a continuous push and pull determining what could and could not be known of the society under study.

(Clifford 1988: 67)

As time went on, though, Griaule began to pursue deeper knowledge of Dogon cosmology, after which Dogon elders agreed to initiate him in the "parole claire" of Dogon philosophy:

Griaule's paradigm of initiation functioned to transform the ethnographer's role from observer and documenter of Dagon culture to exegete and interpreter. It preserved and reformulated, however, the dominant themes of his earlier practice: the logic of the secret, an aspiration to exhaustive knowledge, a vision of fieldwork as role playing. It expressed also the sense one has throughout Griaule's career of his Dogan counterparts as powerful agents in the ethnographic process, initially clever tacticians and willful resisters, later teachers and colleagues. By attaining a parole claire and working like any initiate to grasp the "words" incarnation in the experiential world, Griaule becomes (always in his parallel, "ethnographic" position) one of a restricted group of "doctors" or "metaphysicians" who control and interpret Dogan knowledge. Griaule is an insider, but with a difference. It is as though the Dogon had recognized the need for a kind of cultural ambassador, a qualified representative who would dramatize and defend their culture in the colonial world and beyond. Griaule in any case acted as if this were his role.

(Clifford 1988: 67)

But what kind of collaboration was this? Had Griaule ever given up his role of white colonial locked in a battle to extract ethnographic knowledge from obstinate, conniving "natives"? Were they really his "colleagues"? Were they even collaborating on the same project?

Many of these same questions might be asked of many anthropologists who have "co-authored" with members of communities – George Hunt (Boas), I Madé Kalér (Mead), Ali bin Usmus (Cora Du Bois) (Rosyada 2022). Although praised as "partners" and "friends" by the anthropologist, it would be hard to believe that these collaborations were not steeped in powerful inequalities. At the very least, there is hardly equity in the benefits of these collaborations, with the anthropologist literally building their career on the backs of native informants.

It is not by mistake that Griaule's (later) colleague Jean Rouch is held up as a pioneer in collaborative ethnography, while Griaule is really not (and rightly so). Rouch's work, as Friedman comments, suggests another level of collaboration altogether:

> What is unique about a Rouch-inspired participatory style of filmmaking is that it is self-conscious about the creation of such participatory frameworks and seeks to provide a space within which the film's subjects (both on-screen and off) can negotiate the manner of their own cultural representation. These negotiations are then inscribed in the film, presenting a snapshot of the negotiation process.
>
> (Friedman 2013: 392)

And don't forget the frivolity and joy that appears in that negotiation between Damoure Zika and Lam Abrahima Dia for decades. When people collaborate on Rouch's ethno-fictions, they not only shape those media, but the trace of that collaboration is part of the film. Having that negotiation there acknowledges the complexity of a collaborative relationship, the ways that meanings do not neatly decompose into a single, authoritative account of culture. Not only did Rouch do this with his collaborators, he also acknowledged (and challenged) the nature of collaboration of his colleagues such as Edgar Morin in *Chronicle of a Summer*.

Yet even there, collaboration could be said to be fraught, and, to be sure, the nature of collaboration will shift over time. For example, the visual anthropologist Charles Menzies had planned a deeply collaborative film with Gitxaala people, some related to him:

> Initially we had planned a more collaborative approach. We floated ideas of involving youth, setting up community advisory boards, reviewing footage as it was shot. At one point a cousin, who was involved on the research committee, put a stop to all that. "You do your film," she told me.
>
> (Menzies 2016: 106)

Here, people were unable to commit time to the level of collaboration Menzies had planned, but the decision-making process was still collaborative – ultimately, Menzies continued his work, "working with, and on behalf of, indigenous peoples of the Pacific Northwest" (Menzies 2016: 105). It's just that the nature of that collaboration changed, as it will change for everyone. Even if, as Lassiter has outlined, a collaborative anthropology "revolves first and foremost around an ethical and moral responsibility to consultants," this not does imply that these obligations can be neatly addressed on a spreadsheet – they will shift over time, because of circumstance, ongoing negotiation, and with new revelations (Lassiter 2005: 79). Not acknowledging this at the very least reduces "collaboration" in anthropology to another, empty synonym for "informant" – more seriously, it might disguise the very extractivist logic it is supposed to address.

In other words, saying that multimodal anthropology is inherently "collaborative" does not mean that it is more equitable than other anthropologies, nor does it mean that the work of multimodal anthropology is necessarily in the community's best interest. What it does mean is that multimodality problematizes collaboration. As we write above, what makes "multimedia" different from "multimodal" is that multimodal anthropologies emerge from the perceived experiences, needs, desires, and goals of the community. When one includes games, illustrations, phone apps in a multimodal ethnographic project it should not be because you happen to like these media platforms, but because they seem appropriate in that collaborative moment. "Moment," though, is the correct word, since the grounds for collaboration will shift over and over again over the course of a project and across different projects.

When we think about community partners we've worked with over decades, it is hardly the case that our collaboration has remained static, and as priorities and power relations shift, so must collaboration. The long-term nature of anthropological fieldwork allows that trajectory to occur. We have worked on gentrification pressures with local collaborators in South Baltimore. Those pressures became realities and our community partners declared that gentrification had won. So, the work and power dimensions shift, particularly when housing developers become part of the mix (Collins and Durington 2014). As institutions change, and as the forces of political economy make and re-make our lives, so does that collaboration need to be interrogated for what it means now and what it could be in the future. As Davis warns, "This does not mean, however, that collaborative research is a sure path to harmony or justice. Indeed, rarely are collaborative projects easy. Tensions arise, and this unease has led me to ask: what are the limits of collaboration?" (Davis 2021). In the end, invoking "collaboration" should mean that you are probing those limits, and using that inquiry to renegotiate the nature of your collaboration. This is the heart of collaboration as an ethics, and, as we argue, at the heart of a multimodal anthropology.

Building off of Lassiter's (2005) work, we offer some general principles for ethical collaboration in multimodal anthropology:

1. People are experts. People possess all sorts of expertise – recognized and unrecognized. Working with collaborative partners means first and foremost recognizing and honoring their expertise. Multimodal forms will flow out of this recognition.
2. Anthropologists are facilitators. There is nothing, really, that the anthropologist(s) could do that people in the community could not, given the time and resources. So the role of multimodal anthropology should be to facilitate the work that the community might have done without the anthropologist.
3. Collaboration is enabled through resources. We'll repeat this throughout this book, but the anthropologist needs to bring resources with them. This is generally what is keeping people from accomplishing what they would like to do, and, therefore, resources open the space for collaboration. One must adhere to the principle of debt incurred (Labov 1982).
4. Collaboration needs to be sustained. When we teach ethnographic methods, one of the axioms we teach is that the anthropologist needs to "leave" the field in order to complete their ethnographic work. And while it is certainly true that people need to stop collecting/analyzing/interpreting data in order to finish whatever media they're making, it is not true that you have "left." Multimodal anthropologists have an ethical obligation to remain engaged in the community, and the media they have made in collaboration with the community. Media – now more than ever – moves and changes in the constellation of its networked connections. So while analysis, interpretation, writing, editing, etc., all imply distance, we cannot "leave" in the sense of absenting ourselves from these processes.

Digital Divide

Although the origins of the terms "digital divide" are ambiguous, as a concept, it was starting to be applied to gaps in access to information technology in the 1990s – just as the internet was starting to take shape as a seemingly limitless resource (Collins 2008). Initially applied to people who refused to embrace the "digital future," the term began to take on other meanings, among them a gap in technological access and a gap in knowledge – in other words, to connote inequality (Gunkel 2003). As the "knowledge economy" became more and more invested in IT and digital tools, the digital divide increased – particularly in terms of education and access. Wealthy schools in wealthy nations could teach children programming and give them access to the internet; working class schools and poor nations could not (Compaine 2001). And, parallel to this, "coding camps" and other training programs for under-served populations often appear tokenistic. One can train anyone up, but what does one do without the continued technology access?

Certainly this is still the case. For example, despite a sharp increase in smartphone adoption over the past decade, most people in developing countries don't own one. There are 63% of people in the world today who are internet users, but 3 billion people are otherwise "unconnected" (Kemp 2022). Yet this is much more complicated than merely the presence or absence of a particular technology. For one thing, these "divides" intersect with a great number of other divides, all related to our highly unequal global system, including global literacy (at 87%) access to education, and access to health care.

But while these inequalities are certainly meaningful, they mask other, more nuanced inequalities that don't fall into neat binarisms of rich and poor, "digital native" and "digital immigrant," Global North and Global South. In a wide-ranging, longitudinal survey, Daniel Miller and associates have documented smartphone usage and social media among peoples all over the world, many of whom are oftentimes lumped into the digital "have-nots": working class peoples, rural peoples, developing communities, elderly people (Miller et al. 2021). Perhaps WhatsApp is the predominant social medium, or connectivity is limited, or the smartphone is shared among a household (Forenbacher et al. 2019). Whatever the case, the idea that digital content is only salient in developed countries, or among privileged peoples, is certainly not true. On the other hand, there is also little doubt that digital divides persist and the global inequalities of which they are a part continue – or are even exacerbated in advanced capitalism. The questions here include: what are digital divides today? And how are they salient to the practice of multimodal anthropology? Finally, which digital divides are we considering and attempting to navigate?

People don't have access to the full range of technological possibilities. When the COVID pandemic moved us into remote learning, these digital divides became instantly obvious. Some of our students had no access to a laptop or desktop computer, and they were forced to attend our classes through their phones. Many of our students had terrible internet connections, or lack of access to broadband. Since broadband access in the US is a for-profit enterprise, the companies have little financial incentive to invest in lower-income or low-population areas. Hence, rural and working-class urban neighborhoods have much lower rates of access. In Baltimore, households that lack internet access track nearly perfectly with the racialized cartographic "Black Butterfly" that Lawrence Brown has described (Abell Foundation 2020; Brown 2021).

Generally, this meant that people were thrown back on their smartphones or in public libraries, where they could gain access, but (during COVID) only from the parking lot. In other words, internet access during COVID tracked with race and social class, with many in Baltimore enduring limited access with their smartphone devices. Of course, even those with full access didn't necessarily have equitable access. In Baltimore, Comcast has a de facto monopoly over internet service. During COVID, it began offering a reduced price "Internet Essentials" to nearly 20% of the city's under-served residents, but the internet speeds were so slow that it was impossible for two people to access online courses at the same time (Davis 2021). Sometimes, internet applications themselves can wield a monopoly control over access – and, of course, over questions of meaning and representation. In *Technology of the Oppressed*, Nemer describes a "zero rating" scheme to offer free data to Brazil's favela residents – but only through Facebook, which, for many people, has become synonymous with the internet itself (Nemer 2022: 85).

This digital divide – mediated and structured through corporate capitalism – can also "infect" what had heretofore been non-digital media. Journals, books, and reports are sometimes available for free through public libraries or open access, but they are more often than not paywalled, with "free content" parsed out to consumers unwilling or unable to pay the full cost. Anthropology journals are rarely available in the scaled-down access provided through public libraries. As more and more aspects of social life are reduced to digital applications – education, job searches, banking, shopping – the digital divide grows (Park and Humphry 2019). Not in an absolute sense, but in differences in quality and in speed that continue to penalize people relative to those with more resources. Throughout COVID-era school closings, students may technically have had access to online education, but the limits to interactivity and participation through their inferior internet connections and inadequate devices compound other structural inequalities in education.

The question for us: How do we address these digital divides in multimodal anthropology? There's not going to be one solution. Anthropologists need to consider the expertise of people in the community with regards to a media platform while at the time acknowledging the inequalities that privilege some voices over others. "Solving" a digital divide is beyond the scope of most anthropological work, but we can strive to mediate some of those inequalities by recognizing the expertise that people possess and including that in a design process that is, ultimately, answerable to the community (see Chapter 7 on design).

People don't have time to work on digital projects. When we've gone into communities to help them with archival work, it is invariably elders in the community who are charged with keeping and organizing the documentary history of churches, neighborhoods, and institutions. The results of their tireless efforts are boxed up in church basements and in filing cabinets tucked away in community centers. That is, unless they have been pilfered by a historian looking to collect and sell church artifacts or display them for a lecture (this happens more often than you think). Generally, digitizing these documents is not something that people are willing or able to undertake, and people likewise don't have the skill sets to develop applications and websites that would make these available to a larger public. This is not to say that there aren't people in the community who could do these things, but they are typically engaged with making a living – typically outside of the community. This means that anthropologists have a distinct advantage over community interlocutors, even when their work is participatory and collaborative.

Originally coined by Jo Freeman in 1972, the "tyranny of structurelessness" characterizes the hierarchies that proliferate when decision-making is putatively horizontal but "informal." Ultimately, Freeman argues, unequal structures will emerge in the interstices (Freeman 1972–1973). Jeffrey Juris adapts Freeman's concept in his discussion of electronically mediated social movements premised on horizontal organization and direct democracy (Juris 2008). People who have time and resources to organize will have an incommensurate influence over the shape of a global movement, even if that movement is inimical to hierarchy. In Juris's ethnography, the inequalities emerge in the differences between activists in the Global North and Global South.

There are a number of ways to mitigate these emergent inequalities, among them explicit agreements about decision-making and power-sharing and a willingness to change directions if decision-making processes are becoming lop-sided in favor of the anthropologist (Cizek et al. 2019). Yet, people are often ignored. In the short book *Obfuscation*, Brunton and Nissenbaum describe the ways state actors have drowned out alternative voices by filling social media with unrelated posts and even algorithmically generated nonsense. "In numbers and frequency, such messages can easily dominate a discussion, effectively ruining the platform for a specific audience through overuse – that is, obfuscating through the production of false, meaningless signals" (Brunton and Nissenbaum 2015: 11). This was an effort by a state (in this case, Russia) to suppress dissent. Other, more positive, examples of "obfuscation" can be seen in the efforts of K-pop fans to disrupt right-wing organizing through hijacking their hashtags (Treré and Bonini 2022).

Yet "obfuscation" happens all of the time, even in the absence of proximal, political intent. Go to YouTube. Look up "Greenmount West." The top videos highlight urban crime and real estate – these videos command hundreds of thousands of views. On the other hand, videos on community projects, or on the Greenmount West Community Center, have – at most – a few dozen views. The message of neighborhood solidarity and efforts to combat gentrification with place-based initiatives is not nearly as loud as media-saturated representations of Baltimore as a crime-filled city. It's even worse than this, though. We know that the YouTube algorithm has a propensity for leading users into "echo chambers," magnifying their own political beliefs (Rochert et al. 2020). What this means is that the nearly invisible work of communities is unlikely to even be a first, second, or third recommendation for users. Once they've clicked on a "Baltimore, drugs and violence" video, there is no escape, since the algorithm leads more toward major media sites and, in Baltimore's case, down a rabbit hole of racist representations of the city proffered by Fox News and other right-wing outlets (Ledwich and Zaitsev 2020). The other side to this is the over-representation of real estate videos. Really, YouTube here is an insightful mirror to capitalism in the city, where neighborhoods can only be pathologized or commodified. The community itself, its health, sociality, education, is obscured under the dross of these over-representations.

Working with communities to produce multimodal, anthropological content is challenged by representational regimes that bury the work of communities under more commodified photos, films, and narratives. Yet this is only the beginning of the danger. When community-produced videos of festivals, health fairs, etc., appear alongside images of boarded-up buildings and police cars, the meaning of these community-made contents changes. Or, alternately, multimodal content can be misappropriated into these pathologized regimes. A recent example would be the frequently jarring, critical images in Shae McCoy's "West Baltimore Ruins" (2021). There, the photographer examines the combination of gentrification and abandonment in order to preserve the memories of residents and neighborhoods (McCoy 2021; Snowden and Soderberg 2021). But images of the same homes proliferate on websites "documenting" Baltimore's abandonment in order to justify right-wing policies that privilege suburbs over cities. In a digital age, this just hinges on context. It's the same house, but the meanings could not be more different.

In *Networked Anthropology* (Collins and Durington 2014), we discuss some techniques for addressing these elements of the digital divide. It seems almost impossible to contest "mainstream" media representations – even though corporate-owned social media platforms often give the illusion of more democratic approaches to media. One technique we've embraced is "targeting." Since it is unlikely that multimodal media content produced in our work will be able to directly contest images of Baltimore as a "failing" city, we instead work on content that is directed at audiences that the community we're working in believes might make a difference, including lawmakers, alternative media sites, and non-profits. In addition, we advocate continued monitoring of multimodal media for misappropriations that may occur when right-wing sites may seek to use it for their own purposes. Requests to remove content from sites might be appropriate here as a strategy.

There is also the problem of ownership. When we first started developing a multimodal anthropology, we were enthusiastic promoters of Creative Commons licensing. Creative Commons allows us to "give" people our content while still retaining authorship. In what some have described as a "hack" of US copyright laws, Creative Commons enables creators to share, (re)create, and collaborate, but to do so in ways that mitigate against the tendency of corporations to absorb public domain content into their profit machine. It is a great deal more than an alternative to traditional copyright, however, and Kelty (2008: 259) has described it as "part of a social imaginary of a moral and technical order" that includes ways of working, ways of creating, and ways of utilizing the work of others. In other words, Creative Commons licensing mirrors many of the aspirations of a multimodal anthropology as not just the multiplication of media and platforms in anthropology, but a challenge to the ways that anthropology has been organized, practiced, and rendered.

Of course, this may not be enough. We were doing work over the summer of 2022 with a community partner who is a savvy media producer – and one comfortable in a variety of platforms. Yet this person was not especially enthusiastic about documenting their work on social media – whether through Creative Commons licensing or something else. When a community has been subject to intellectual theft (as well as many other forms of material and immaterial violence), we may find people loath to "give away" anything. The chance of theft and co-optation is too dire, and the memory of working on something only to see it "invented" by a more affluent, usually white outsider is still fresh in the minds of many in the communities where we work. This is also the case in many parts of the world, where the art, music, pharmacopeia, and cosmologies of many communities have been violently appropriated into a profit machine, with none of the appropriated profits going to the communities where these ideas and practices originated.

There are other possibilities, including "TK" Licenses, which are a way of exerting control over content that might otherwise be appropriated as "traditional" media. Notions of single ownership, and, more broadly, reifications common to capitalism that extend copyright control to a "work" decontextualized from culture and social life, may not be in the best interests of many communities, hence the development of a TK License that is "aimed specifically at the complex intellectual property needs of indigenous peoples, communities, and collectivities wishing to manage, maintain, and preserve their digital cultural heritage in relation to multiple sets of rights and stakeholder obligations" (Anderson and Christen 2013: 111). On the other hand, the people we collaborate with may need to monetize what they do in order to survive in a capitalist world – and this should be something that we support as well. In fact, we would encourage practitioners to challenge their university lawyers with working a Creative Commons license or an alternative form of intellectual ownership into a contract or honorarium. Why not? We have.

Finally, questions of ownership and intellectual property do not just boil down to who owns what, or how content will be re-used later on, but really involve an accounting of previous inequality, and the possibility for more equity in the future. No matter how altruistic the anthropology or benevolent the cause, if we do not both acknowledge the past and contribute to a more equitable future, we are failing in the ethical practice of multimodal anthropology.

Conclusion

If anthropology is the sum of its ethics, then new methods in anthropology mean new ethical orientations. And while we have argued that multimodal anthropology is not "new" in the sense of a decisive break with the past, the emphasis on non-textual content and participatory media mean that certain ethical relationships and obligations rise to the fore – alongside the more well-known ethical mores in the field to do no harm, to practice transparency, and so on. If we were to visualize this re-shuffling of anthropological ethics, it might look something like the chart in Figure 2.2.

Ethics, here, is about the contexts that frame every stage of anthropological work, from initial research through to the ways multimodal works are framed in their re-use and citation. And all of this is part of ethnographic work as an iterative process.

Classroom Exercise

One of the themes in this chapter has been the inevitability of ethical questions, even if those questions will differ according to the platform. In this exercise, students mine their own media usage for its ethical orientations.

1   Have students document their media use – including digital and analog forms.
2   Have students imagine ethnographic projects where these media would be used as part of the research process or research dissemination.
3   Have students brainstorm on ethical dilemmas, including questions of access and equity, privacy and use, ownership and monetization.
4   Imagine a worst-case scenario relating to a particular medium. How might students approach this as anthropologists? At what point would this research be too ethically problematic to continue?

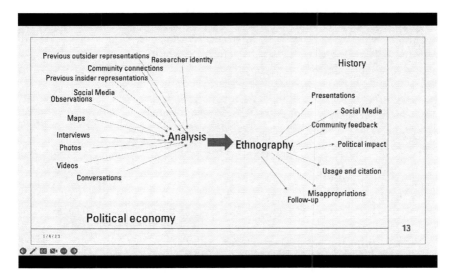

Figure 2.2 Reshuffling anthropological ethics

References

Abell Foundation. (2020). *Baltimore's digital divide: Gaps in internet connectivity and the impact on low-income city residents.* Abell Foundation.

Anderson, J., & Christen, K. (2013). "Chuck a copyright on it": Dilemmas of digital return and the possibilities for traditional knowledge licenses and labels. *Museum Anthropology Review*, 7,(1–2), 105–126.

Annas, G.J. (2006). Anthropology, IRB, and human rights. *American Ethnologist*, 33 (4), 541–544.

Astacio, P.A., Dattatreyan, E.G., & Shankar, A. (2021). Multimodal ambivalence. *American Anthropologist*, 123(2), 420–430.

Boas, F. (1919). Scientists as spies. *The Nation*, 109(2842), 1.

Bozeman, B., & Hirsch, P. (2006). Science ethics as a bureaucratic problem. *Policy Sciences*, 38, 269–291.

Brown, L. (2021). *Black Butterfly*. Johns Hopkins Press.

Brunton, F., & Nissenbaum, H. (2016). *Obfuscation*. MIT Press.

Caplan, P. (2003). Introduction. In P. Caplan (ed.), *The ethics of anthropology*. Routledge, pp. 1–345.

Chin, E. (2017). On multimodal anthropologies from the space of design: Toward participant making. *American Anthropologist*, 119(3), 541–546.

Cizek, K., Uricchio, W., Massiah, L., Mertes, C., & Winger-Bearskin, A. (2019). Part 2: How to co-create: Practical lessons from the field. In *Collective Wisdom* (1st edn). MIT Press.

Clifford, J. (1988). *The predicament of culture: Twentieth-century ethnography, literature, and art*. Harvard University Press. https://doi.org/10.2307/j.ctvjf9x0h.

Cole, R. (2018). Mastery and masquerade in the transatlantic blues revival. *Journal of the Royal Musical Association*, 143(1), 173–210.

Collins, S.G. (2008). *All tomorrow's cultures: Anthropological engagements with the future*. Berghahn Books.

Collins, S.G., & Durington, M. (2014). *Networked anthropology: A primer for ethnographers*. Routledge.

Compaine, B. (2001). *The digital divide: Facing a crisis or creating a myth?* MIT Press.

Davis, P. (2021). Comcast, under pressure from politicians and advocates, raises speeds of Internet Essentials service. *Baltimore Sun*, February 2. www.baltimoresun.com/politics/bs-md-ci-van-hollen-comcast-internet-20210202-drxyymiqavh23iwa4ksyreq63i-story.html.

Forenbacher, I., Husnjak, S., Cvitić, I., & Jovovic, I. (2019). Determinants of mobile phone ownership in Nigeria. *Telecommunications Policy*, 43. DOI: doi:10.1016/j.telpol.2019.03.001.

Freeman, J. (1972–1973). The tyranny of structurelessness. *Berkeley Journal of Sociology*, 17, 151–164.

Friedman, P.K. (2013). Collaboration against ethnography. *Critique of Anthropology*, 33(4), 391–411.

Gunkel, D.J. (2003). Second thoughts: Toward a critique of the digital divide. *New Media & Society*, 5(4), 499–522. https://doi.org/10.1177/146144480354003.

Jobson, R.C. (2020). The case for letting anthropology burn. *American Anthropologist*, 122(2), 259–271.

Juris, J. (2008). *Networking futures*. Duke University Press.

Kelty, C. (2008). *Two bits*. Duke University Press.

Kemp, S. (2022). Datareportal. https://datareportal.com/reports/digital-2022-global-overview-report.
Labov, W. (1982). Objectivity and commitment in linguistic science: The case of the Black English trial in Ann Arbor. *Language in Society*, 11(2), 165–201. www.jstor.org/stable/4167310.
Lassiter, L. (2005). Collaborative ethnography and public anthropology. *Current Anthropology*, 46(1), 83–106. https://doi.org/10.1086/425658.
Ledwich, M., & Zaitsev, A. (2020). Algorithmic extremism: Examining YouTube's rabbit hole of radicalization. *First Monday*. https://firstmonday.org/article/view/10419/9404.
McCoy, S. (2021). West Baltimore ruins. www.shaemccoyphotography.com/west-baltimore-ruins.
Menzies, C. (2016). *People of the saltwater: An ethnography of Git lax m'oon*. University of Nebraska Press.
Miller, D., Rabho, L.A., Awondo, P., de Vries, M., Duque, M., Garvey, P., Haapio-Kirk, L., Hawkins, C., Otaegui, A., Walton, S., & Wang, X. (2021). *The global smartphone*. UCL Press.
Nemer, D. (2022). *Technology of the oppressed*. MIT Press.
Park, S., & Humphry, J. (2019). Exclusion by design: Intersections of social, digital and data exclusion. *Information, Communication & Society*, 22, 934–953. DOI: doi:10.1080/1369118X.2019.1606266.
Pels, P. (1999). Professions of duplexity. *Current Anthropology*, 40(2), 101–130.
Plattner, S. (2006). Comment on IRB Regulation of ethnographic research. *American Ethnologist*, 33(4), 525–528.
Rochert, D., Neubaum, G., Ross, B., Brachten, F., & Stieglitz, S. (2020). Opinion-based homogeneity on YouTube: Combining sentiment and social network analysis. *Computational Communication Research*, 2(1), 81–108. https://doi.org/10.5117/%20CCR2020.1.004.ROCH.
Rosyada, A. (2022). Unsung native collaborators in anthropology. *Sapiens*. www.sapiens.org/culture/native-collaborators-anthropology-mead-boas/.
Shange, S. (2016). Collaboration: Implication. *Cultural Anthropology*. https://culanth.org/fieldsights/collaboration-implication.
Shange, S. (2022). Abolition in the clutch. *Feminist Anthropology*, 3, 187–197.
Snowden, L., & Soderberg, B. (2021). "West Baltimore ruins" preserves the memory of neglected neighborhoods before they're lost to gentrification. *The Real News Network*. https://therealnews.com/west-baltimore-ruins-preserves-the-memory-of-neglected-neighborhoods-before-theyre-lost-to-gentrification.
Takaragawa, S., Smith, T.L., Hennessy, K., Alvarez Astacio, P., Chio, J., Nye, C., & Shankar, S. (2019). Bad Habitus: Anthropology in the age of the multimodal. *American Anthropologist*, 121, 517–524. https://doi.org/10.1111/aman.13265.
Tierney, P. (2001). *Darkness in El Dorado*. W.W. Norton.
Treré, E., & Bonini, T. (2022). Amplification, evasion, hijacking: Algorithms as repertoire for social movements and the struggle for visibility. *Social Movement Studies*. DOI: doi:10.1080/14742837.2022.2143345.

3 Photography

Multimodality begins when we start to genuinely collaborate with the communities where we do our research. This wasn't always the case though. In early anthropological practice the documentation of collaboration through text never really occurred despite the reality of fieldwork dynamics. We often use the metaphor of imagining Clifford Geertz just hovering omniscient above Bali where everything occurring would be happening even if he wasn't there. Yet of course he is there but the idea of Geertz floating is still fun. The anthropologist is present. The collaborator(s) are also present. So, how is the anthropologist conducting research if it is not in collaboration? The collaborator has been conceived as subject, or even worse, primitive, savage, or barbarian. Perhaps no other medium used in anthropology by early anthropologists exacerbated this bias and othering practice than photography. It literally froze people in time, and add the notion of time philosophically to these images and you have a template for othering (Fabian 2014). Images certainly did not do anything to dispel the exotic reification of those the anthropologist was working with. In the 20th century as photography became an established practice and tool in the field, anthropologists pulled on different theories of visual communication, deliberations over the power of text and image, and began to look back to critically analyze the use of photography and photographic representations. Anthropologists also began to think about images in their theoretical grounding and research methodology. As we document in this chapter, participatory action research and photovoice are examples where photography is integrated into collaborative multimodal practice, although it does not completely solve representational dilemmas. Photography may be a certain form of seeing and representation, but it's one with a long history of community negotiation, exchange and redeployment toward a variety of purposes. This chapter also considers the fates of these photovoice projects in exhibits, online, and elsewhere. And we project how multimodal practice can continue to utilize photography in discursive analysis and practice.

Perhaps no other medium other than note taking on paper has been a representational tool of the ethnographic fieldwork experience than photography. This medium epitomizes the tensions of whether the photographs of

DOI: 10.4324/9781003330851-4

fieldwork activities, peoples, and other things in the anthropological encounter are empirical evidence or are research in and of themselves. Photography is proof of *in situ* fieldwork to affirm presence and authority that derives from it in ethnographic documentation. Yet, "pictures can't say ain't." While discussing the work of Sol Worth, Eco made this eloquent statement to point out that pictures cannot display absence (Gross 1980). They can only show what is present. Or, what is presented. And, when one looks at the fieldwork photos of historical anthropology they often appear to be neatly arranged in a very colonial fashion. They are picked purposefully to show what the anthropologist wants the viewer to see as the intended representation of their work. They also impart an implicit and explicit power dynamic. They do not necessarily show signs of modernity that would interfere with the anthropological imagination of what is reified in front of the lens. Thus, while pictures can be telling, they can't convey absence – the absence of context and collaboration. This is despite the fact that photographs are often held up as irrefutable proof of presence. This has not changed as photography has become easier with software, modern cameras, and smartphones. We are now more selective about what we want represented than ever before. The expression "photoshopped" connotes absence of what is real. Ask any Kardashian. Smartphones will literally create extraction and absence with tools such as Google's "magic" tool or Apple's IOS 16. Your annoying brother in law ruins the family photo? Simply extract them. One could almost speculate that absence and extraction are a form of interpretive violence. It may also produce a "scopic viscerality" as seen in the photographs of Jeffrey Schronberg in the photo-ethnography *Righteous Dopefiend* (Durington and Demyan 2012).

Thus, when discussing anthropology and photography through a multimodal lens (pun intended) we must situate any so-called objective understanding gleaned from the analysis of a photograph with the understanding that it is incapable of objectivity. This line of inquiry opens up many of the possibilities that a multimodal approach provides by starting to ask questions about presence, absence, process, reflexivity, and collaboration. We have argued previously for a lack of aesthetics in visual anthropology with the supposition that when a film is too aesthetically pleasing, it may be lacking something. We once again turn to Jean Rouch as an example for letting the reality of a situation trump the aesthetic choice. Rouch and his compatriots were masters of staged reality by revealing the process of staging it. The often jovial process of ethno-fiction creates a more robust objectivity because it emphasizes process and reflexivity to create representation. This begs the question that we often pose for students in visual anthropology or multimodal sections of our curriculum. What is more loaded with meaning? Is it the moving image through film and video? Or, is it the still image? There is no doubt that as Nanook is biting the phonograph record in *Nanook of the North* one presupposes his lack of understanding of that technology.

58 *Photography*

But hey, it's a good gag, right? Why make Nanook look out of time? What other signs of modernity may have been out of shot? We do see Robert Flaherty in Figure 3.1.

While some have just used this picture to talk about *Nanook of the North* without any critical interrogation (Rotha 1980), Ruby argues for further contextualization As he states in the introduction to that published piece as editor, "Our interests have shifted from the 'text' to the 'context' as being of primary importance" (Ruby 1980: 2). So here we are at the importance of context. What is going on around the photographic moment? What is outside of the photographic shot, particularly if one is attempting to empirically represent ethnographic work or convey anthropological meaning? Or what new meaning can be created by manipulating the photograph to project an intended purpose? As seen in Figures 3.2 and 3.3, it is obvious that Durington was with Bateson and Mead as they conducted fieldwork.

These are the critical interpretive dilemmas that make photography and anthropology so exciting. Our assertion is that simply taking a picture to illustrate what is going on during fieldwork or as an exemplar of experience is actually quite boring. It's much more interesting to look at the practice of photography and the actual images created and interrogate them in a multimodal fashion. Since the late days of the 19th century and throughout the 20th century photography has been seen as an established research tool in anthropology. It has been seen as a way to document culture and as a means of communicating the intention of anthropologists to an audience. Does a

Figure 3.1 Nanook "biting" a record

Photography 59

Figure 3.2 Matthew Durington greenscreen

Figure 3.3 Matthew Durington conducting fieldwork in Bali with Margaret Mead and Gregory Bateson

60 Photography

Figure 3.4 The treachery of images; "This Is Not a Pipe" by Rene Magritte

picture require text to interpret it? It's a classic argument, as illustrated in Figure 3.4. Or, does the picture have the capacity to stand on its own as research in and of itself? Is the picture data? Are we trapped in a conundrum that Magritte provides us when he states "Ceci n'est pas une pipe" challenging the power of language, objects, and representational meaning in images?

Photography in Early Science and Pseudoscience

Early scientists including both those working with newly established methodological guidelines as well as practitioners of many pseudosciences saw photography as a mechanism for capturing objective reality – at least, a reality that confirmed problematic assumptions of other peoples. The father of the eugenics pseudoscience, Francis Galton, used pictures as early as 1878, referring to photography as a tool to create "generic mental images," better known as stereotypes of various populations. Galton went as far as creating a methodology of aligning individuals in composite imagery based on axes of pupils and other facial features (see Figure 3.5). Of course, this so-called empirical tool was altered and shaped to reinforce the Eurocentric archetypes that Galton elevated as ideal while also using it to designate sufferers of various maladies. Perhaps most famous is Galton's array of criminal types that influenced a variety of fields into the 20th century, and which one could argue continues to influence criminology. In order to study and depict so-called "others" in the late 19th century, one only needed a solid assumption about the superiority of European civilization, a pair of calipers, and a graphed background for scantily clad folks to stand in front of the camera. What's the most important aspect of this reflection? It's not the photographs themselves, but the speculation on the context in which they were taken, and the way in which they have been utilized in a problematic way historically.

Photography 61

Figure 3.5 Composite criminality, Francis Galton

Juxtaposed to Galton we have the work of Jacob Riis and his attempts to humanize tenement life in an era where immigrants were being positioned as sub-human, or even as a different species. Whereas the anthropomorphic work of Galton and others was attempting to situate criminality and associate it with various others through photography, Riis was using photography to show the living conditions of the poor in New York City in order to position their humanity (for example see Figure 3.6). Juxtapose the photos of Galton and Riis as an intellectual or even multimodal exercise and the differences between the two intentions becomes readily apparent. The use of photographs by Riis was meant to illustrate his writings about the abhorrent conditions of tenements, and to sway public opinion about housing conditions among immigrants in New York which led to concrete social reforms in housing and sanitation laws. As others have noted there is all kinds of context around Riis, his practice, and photography (Chan 2008).

For this exercise let's ask more questions. Is Riis an applied anthropologist that used his visual methods toward changing social policy? No, but can we look at *How the Other Half Lives* as a means to disrupt problematic assertions about immigrants through photography used by Galton? Yes. Is there plenty to pick apart with Riis and the project? Sure. Can we talk about economies of circulation? Can we talk about purported objectivity through photography? Can we talk about the cultural context of intense racism through both examples? Indeed. It is the interrogation of cultural context that is both anthropological and multimodal. And, what is most fascinating is the idea of truth or realness. Google "are Frank Riis images real" and see what happens. Do the same for Galton.

Perhaps no image represents American anthropology more than Franz Boas in anthropomorphic regalia posing to illustrate certain poses related to his work among the Hamats'a. As Alex Golub has noted, these images now archived by the Smithsonian have become "memeworthy in extremis" (Golub 2018), and are used in countless classrooms and jokes in the field. The fact that "Papa Franz" is also seen as the father of American anthropology proves the connection between photography and anthropology since the relativistic turn in

62 *Photography*

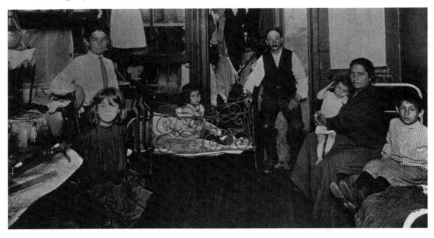

Figure 3.6 How the Other Half Lives, Jacob Riis

the discipline. Whereas the photograph in Figure 3.7 is definitely the most memeworthy, the picture in Figure 3.8 is the one we prefer the most.

Why the second one? Well, it is because it captures that crazed look of someone who wanted to regard a culture on its own terms, diversify the field of practicing anthropologists, and argue that race is a cultural construction. Can you put this photo on a projector and start to unpack that context? We like both because they are copyright free. And the Hamats'a series by Boas for the American National Museum emphasizes a process

Figure 3.7 Franz Boas, anthropomorphic study, *Hamats'a Coming Out of Secret Room* Photo 1

Photography 63

Figure 3.8 Franz Boas, anthropomorphic study, *Hamats'a Coming Out of Secret Room* Photo 2

using photography and kinesics. They are beautifully imperfect just as that time in anthropology was... with the necessary contemporary interrogation. While this may seem like cherry picking when you consider the anthropometric extension of Boas's work with the Jesup Expedition, we can still look to Boas for the attempt with that work to challenge the credibility of racialized theories being used against Jewish populations in Europe (Maxwell 2013). But perhaps our favorite multimodal extension of the Hamats'a photos of Boas and the Boas persona is found with the powerhouse faculty of the anthropology department who have taken these images and translated them into t-shirts, mugs, and even masks during COVID in a jovial fashion. Note the "three howl Boas" adorning the t-shirt in Figure 3.9. Walter Benjamin would be proud.

We even got permission from the powerhouse faculty of The Anthropology Department to use the image in Figure 3.10.

Edward Curtis is well known in anthropology for the massive representational corpus of Native American populations in *The North American Indian* (Curtis 1999). Over 30 years Curtis documented dozens of Native American populations that became part of this 20 volume publication. The circulation of these images is perhaps the most fascinating aspect of the body of work. Curtis experimented with different cameras and printing techniques and aesthetically the photographs are often noted for their

64 *Photography*

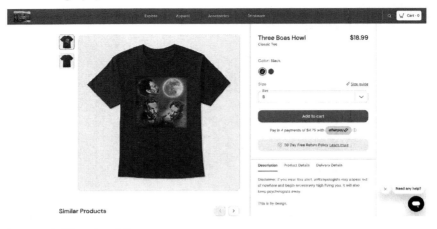

Figure 3.9 Three howl Boas

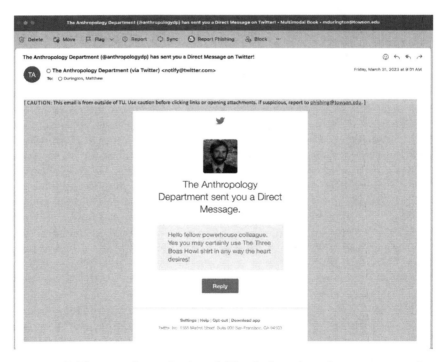

Figure 3.10 The powerhouse faculty of The Anthropology Department granting permission via social media

beauty. While the photographs of Curtis are heralded for contradicting some of the problematic perceptions of Native Americans in popular culture, he is also criticized for romanticizing this culture and bolstering notions of "the noble savage." From a multimodal perspective, it is the staging and manipulation of scenes that is most interesting. What was going on as the photographs were being staged? Were conversations taking place collaboratively to depict certain actions over others? George Hunt was definitely in the mix, right (Glass 2009)? Gidley's take on the work of Edward Curtis is that while these photos are beautiful, they definitely contributed to a reifying of Native American populations as noble savages and falsely justifying in turn the marginalization of these groups (Gidley 2006).

Aaron Glass has explored the images, films, and dynamics of Edward Curtis through several exploratory pieces (Glass 2009). Glass discusses how these photographs construct and obscure culture realities in the way in which they are circulated and interpreted amongst the public and within Native American cultures themselves. In later explorations, Glass and Evans undertake an incredible comprehensive evaluation of Curtis's famous film *In the Land of the Headhunters*. This project brings together authors from a number of disciplines to re-examine and critically evaluate the place of this

Figure 3.11 George Hunt, 1893
Source: Photographed by Gibson, Jackson Park, Chicago. (Courtesy of Courtesy of Harvard University Archives, Frederic Ward Putnam Papers)

film in representational history of the Kwakwaka'wakw and Native American representations. While artists, film critics, and anthropologists offer their perspectives on this body of work, Glass and Evans take pains to ensure that the agency and voices of Kwakwaka'wakw are represented as well (Evans and Glass 2014). The collection of essays demonstrates that Curtis distinctively staged his representations but nonetheless they contain ethnographic meaning, or data, even though these images are mediated in different ways over time. The usage of photography by both anthropologists and those being depicted by the camera is the complicated analysis that a multimodal approach demands.

Photography Theory and Methodology

Once again, we look back to the journal *Studies in Visual Communication* for a multimodal reclamation of theory and speculation. In the seminal article "Photography and Sociology," Howard Becker positions photography as a tool for sociological research due to its ability to capture social life that can be analyzed later in research (Becker 1974). This assertion of the photograph as evidence and data that can be analyzed for research was not uncommon then, nor is it today. Yet, Becker was in conversations with many of the individuals that we have highlighted thus far and from these conversations one can speculate on a multimodal approach to photography. For Becker, and us, it's not so much that "Pictures can't say ain't," or that pictures are understood to represent objective reality. Rather, it is the primacy of the social context in which the picture is taken that is paramount. One must contemplate the perspective of the photographer, the cultural context in which the photograph was taken, and last but not least, the ways in which the photograph is used and analyzed. William Ivins also speaks to the power of photography through prints to convey complex information with an emphasis on cultural context (Ivins 1969). These elements of subjectivity, context, and usage emphasize process. They allow us to move away from whether or not a picture is "good" or "bad." A striking photograph is a wonderful thing to view but these aesthetic evaluations are somewhat meaningless to a multimodal approach. We would be more interested in what the photographer was thinking when the picture was taken, what was going on when it happened, and then later contemplate how it is analyzed and used. In a perfect world, we would understand the meaning created in collaboration between the photographer and the person being represented. These are the elements that underlie the collaborative process of participatory methodology in photovoice.

Any discussion of the history and practice of anthropology and photography is a massive undertaking but we want to consider the same reclamation project that a multimodal approach provides us when we look at the past. There is a definite parallel between the history of both photography and anthropology (Pinney 2011). While visual anthropology is often equated with ethnographic film, when one considers the expanse of visual accompaniment to anthropological work throughout time the primacy of photography is readily apparent. In its early iterations photography was appreciated for its supposed capacity of providing a permanent record of an event or place when a language barrier or speech was in existence or fieldnotes considered less objective (Pinney 2011). As noted, elder figures to the field such as Franz Boas employed photography as part of their methodology in lock step with traditional approaches to fieldwork. Boas used photography on his first field trip to Baffinland in 1883 (Jacknis 1984). While the use of photography by Boas and other progenitors of the field was not intended to exotify indigenous cultures, much of that early work is considered to be Eurocentric and evidence of a colonial past in the discipline (Edwards 1994). Photography was relied upon for its capacity to supposedly capture objective reality of cultures that were seen as under threat by modernity. While the potential exoticism that emerges in photographing indigenous populations is now critically approached in anthropology, other entities such as *National Geographic* continued to follow a cultural salvage approach throughout most of the 20th century (Lutz and Collins 1993). *National Geographic* only recently admitted in a special series that the publication was racist and promoted caricatures of indigenous peoples and others (Greenfield 2018).

A parallel argument for the supposed objectivity of photography can be found in the use of ethnographic film in anthropology. As Ruby has noted, the use of film was considered to have similar attributes to create the so-called scientific record of the anthropological fieldwork process or serve as an objective piece of evidence (Ruby 1982). In this sense, film was considered to be the *trompe l'oeil* of anthropological work with the power of bringing populations to life for an anthropological audience. The naiveté of this approach became the fodder for postmodern critiques of the visual. As Ruby notes, "The belief that film can be an unmediated record of the real world is based on the idea that cameras, not people, take pictures and the naive empiricist notion that the world is as it appears to be" (Ruby 1982: 125).

But even in this naïve empiricism, photography could also be collaborative. An important book in the recognition of photography as a research tool was the publication of *Visual Anthropology: Photography as a Research Method*. Authored by John and Malcolm Collier, this landmark publication is the touchstone for any syllabus or publication that attempts to discuss photography and its merits.

Photo elicitation is an important and widely used methodological tool that is relied upon for its simplicity. John Collier actually coined the term photo elicitation in 1957 asserting the importance of using photography to elicit information and insights from collaborators in anthropology (Collier 1957). For Collier, photo elicitation is relied upon in anthropological fieldwork to create discussion, reflections and to understand the cultural context of individuals. It's a straightforward approach that can produce complex information. As Harper states, "Photo elicitation is based on the simple idea of inserting a photograph into a research interview" (Harper 2002: 13). Harper also looks to Rouch and others in visual anthropology for their use of film as an elicitation technique with Morin and Rouch being leaders for their work in the landmark film *Chronicle of a Summer*. Durington has used photo elicitation as a research tool in his work on suburban teenage heroin overdose populations where one single image from a newspaper became the catalyst for a moral panic in the Dallas suburb of Plano, Texas in 1998 (Durington 2007). This image appeared in countless places throughout the fieldwork site and was used by parents, educators, medical professionals, law enforcement, and others as a touchstone to elicit reaction from an audience. Referred to as the "dead kids list," Durington discusses how he was able to not only elicit reactions from collaborators as part of interviews, but also discursively analyze the circulation of the image during the moral panic. And, as we have asserted as well, there is nothing more productive than asking a collaborator to show you their photo albums or home movies and that these media deserve ethnographic attention just as much as anything produced by an anthropologist.

One of the strongest tenets of a multimodal approach is a focus on collaboration. If one were to look for a multitude of multimodal projects that center collaboration in their methodology and outcomes, participatory action research (PAR) is a rich repository, one that we follow into a discussion of participatory design in Chapter 7. Gubrium, Harper and Otañez collected many elements of this work in the collection of essays in *Participatory Visual and Digital Research in Action* (2015). The table of contents speaks to many of the practices we have attempted to assert as multimodal work since 2017 and that structure this book including digital storytelling, photovoice, participatory video, participatory mapping, participatory archive work, and participatory design ethnography. Krista Harper has been a champion of bringing multimodal elements to ethnographic and participatory work throughout her career as have many others. PAR is based on collaboration between researchers and community collaborators. In this work, the voices and intentions of collaborators guides the entire process from beginning to the interpretive end. The intention is to both recognize and bolster the agency of collaborators. Elements of PAR work emphasize collaboration with goals of empowerment and action with a built-in reflexive process as part of dissemination.

All PAR projects tend to involve a common desire to work with collaborators to address "real-world" situations (Greenwood and Levin 1998). In our National Science Foundation project "Anthropology by the Wire" we set out to conduct PAR research with multimedia in 2011. While much has changed technologically, the principles that guided this initial work nevertheless led us to theorizing a *Networked Anthropology* and now a *Multimodal Anthropology*. This work involved training students in methods and ethics and creating research teams to walk through Baltimore neighborhoods using mapping and photography. This is followed by photo elicitation interviews with each other and eventually with collaborators in these spaces. Our goal with this photo elicitation was for students to reflect on their perceptions of "the city" and connect it to PAR they were conducting (Harper 2002; Kedia and van Willigen 2005). Students then compare their representations with mass media depictions of the City of Baltimore which are highly problematic and then, in turn, use these as prompts with community collaborators. This process truly becomes alive when photographs are used as guideposts for "transect walks" with collaborators through their neighborhoods. This creates a strong collaborative process where our students use photos in unstructured interviews to glean further information from collaborators leading to discussions of what needs to be done to address inequities and other socioeconomic issues in these communities. Other PAR methods utilizing the collection of photos are "scanathons" where community members gather historic photos which are then scanned by researchers and given back in a digital archive to participants. The process of the scanathon, based on the collection of photos, creates a transformative encounter and is the impetus for further research.

The most recognized and utilized PAR tool with photography is photovoice. Simply put, photovoice is a participatory method that uses photography with the purpose of generating critical discussions in concert with marginalized communities to address a number of issues. The process involves distributing cameras, asking collaborators to document with an intention, and then create an event where said photographs are analyzed and discussed. Originally coined by Wang and Burris as a concept in the 1990s, there are precedents in various fields (including anthropology) that sought to utilize this type of methodology in participatory methods (Wang and Burris 1997). There is a consensus across disciplines that photovoice combines photographs, discussion, contextual knowledge, and a collaborative environment in order to reflect on experiences, communicate issues, and discuss possibilities of social change. It has been used in dozens of fields on dozens of projects. Krista Harper has become a leader in this methodology in anthropology through projects addressing food justice in urban school systems (Harper et al. 2017), gardening with fifth graders (Sands et al. 2009), and environment and health in Romani communities (Harper et al. 2009).

Sometimes, however, photovoice projects have not lived up to the promise of the method, and, indeed, some recapitulate the power inequalities of earlier periods of documentary photography. Shankar provides a "gentle" critique of the photovoice method by noting that the uncritical use of photovoice "has allowed a reinvigoration of a positivist orientation toward image authenticity and… inadvertently supports hegemonic regimes of value" (Shankar 2016: 157). He further argues that participants in photovoice projects must be considered as "auteurs producing realities" (Shankar 2016: 157). This notion of agency further emboldens the ethnographic merit of media being produced by our interlocutors while complicated by the explosion of photographic technology and the ubiquity of cameras. Just because the camera has become more accessible does not necessarily translate to more productive photovoice projects though.

As alluded to in Shankar's critique of photovoice, these projects can often become "cringy" when claims are made that these projects give "voice to the voiceless" or directly create change. These notions align with neoliberalism and often reek of the white savior industrial complex. Want to do something about poverty? Let's do a photovoice project and worry about structural violence later. If these claims of direct solutions are made in a project one should proceed with caution. Rather, photovoice projects should lead to further interrogations and speculations and not be seen as solutions in and of themselves. They can be incredibly revelatory for participants and audiences, but for how long? What happens past the gallery exhibition when the project is displayed for the first time? These are usually the events where a dialogue can occur between participants, researchers, and possibly an audience. A multimodal approach would only begin with the training of participants, the process of taking photos, the selection of images, and the installation in a gallery-type setting. It is the conversations and processes that would become primary for a multimodal anthropology. The speculative collaborative outcomes have merit, but too often we retreat into aesthetics and determine if a photo is "good" or "bad," particularly past the gallery opening when photos are displayed with a lack of direct context. Furthermore, we have to ask ourselves why we are drawn to photovoice projects with particular communities in the first place. The *raison d'etre* for photovoice projects is marginalization. Are these projects developed to ameliorate marginalization? One would not do it otherwise and a multimodal ethics demands that those rationales must be contextualized, especially in public health where photovoice projects could easily slip into exploitation.

Conclusion

So what about those photos in the family albums sitting in the corner of the living room bookshelf while you are interviewing a collaborator about their life? Are they meritorious of ethnographic speculation? Any visual anthropologist worth their photo elicitation *bona fides* would say absolutely yes. But, would that same visual anthropologist consider those photos in and of themselves ethnographic? Is that an anthropological bridge too far since these individuals are not professional anthropologists with credentials? One of the longest arguments that has engaged, or perhaps plagued, visual anthropology is who has the capacity to produce visual anthropology, particularly in the form of ethnographic film. No less than Jay Ruby asserted that only someone who is academically trained as a professional anthropologist possesses adequate production skills and is competent enough to produce something that is ethnographic media (Ruby 2000). We empathize with this to some degree. Many individuals claim that they are doing "visual anthropology" simply by pointing the camera toward an individual deemed exotic, racialized, and if it all works out clad in something resembling traditional dress while doing traditional things.

But Ruby's approach to ethnographic authority has also been ambiguous. In the 1991 essay "Speaking for, speaking about, speaking with, or speaking alongside: An anthropological and documentary dilemma," Ruby begins with dialogue from the 1975 film *The Passenger* to question where authorial agency lies in visual productions. As Ruby questions this agency he appears to lend some credence to the ethnographic capacity of media produced by those who are not actually trained as anthropologists to ascertain culture:

> Cooperatively produced and subject-generated films are significant because they represent an approach to documentary and ethnographic films dissimilar to the dominant practice. They offer the possibility of perceiving the world from the viewpoint of the people who lead lives that are different from those traditionally in control of the means for imaging the world. Subject-generated films and video are a tool used by some disenfranchised people in their efforts to negotiate a new cultural identity. For other indigenous and minority producers, making movies and television is a way into the profits and power of the established order.
>
> (Ruby 1991: 50)

Transpose this argument to photography and you get the picture (again, pun intended). We continue to emphasize the importance of collaboration, cultural context, and the recognition of agency as pillars of a multimodal practice. We also recognize the importance of circulation and usage of photographs to generate meaning. But perhaps more than anything, it is the experimentation with photography that pushes multimodalities. A common assumption is that a multimodal photographic practice would include various expository components such as interviews, captions, etc. When we assumed the position as editors of the multimodal section in *American Anthropologist* we asked a very simple question: can we just publish a photograph? One can imagine the response from the powers that be at the publishing juggernaut that controlled all of the American Anthropological Association journals at that point. Yet, we pushed and pushed until we convinced the powers that be to publish *Tainted Frictions: A Visual Essay* by Paolo Favero (2017). While Favero provides interpretive context for the published photo, it is meant to be a series of guideposts for interpreting the image. As Favero states:

> Tainted Frictions is a non-linear visual essay that produces a generative set of tensions between photography and text. The essay contains two parallel tracks bringing content in dialogue with form. On the one hand it addresses (mainly with the help of original photographs taken in India and Cuba by the author) the meaning of colour in the contact zone between the colonizers and the colonized. On the other hand, it offers a (formal) challenge to conventional ways of presenting social scientific research. Aiming to offer a vision about a possible future for

the photo-essay Tainted Frictions suspends consolidated (hierarchical) ways of bringing text and image in contact with each other (hence going beyond "the caption").

(Favero 2017: 361)

The essay is unique in that the photos themselves are not necessarily the subject of the "essay," but rather it is the process of interpreting it that moves it into a different multimodal space.

As far as we know it is the first of its kind to come with interpretive instructions as seen below:

How to interact with the essay:
In order to explore this visual essay do the following steps:
#1. Download the PDF or JPG file.
#2. Open it up with an image viewing software (Preview, Image Viewer, etc.).
#3. You are now ready to start swimming in the image.

(Favero 2017: 364)

We also look to our colleagues who formed and executed the decade-plus project Ethnographic Terminalia as a massive repository for multimodal experimentation with photography. In 2016, the collective ran a workshop entitled "The photo-essay is dead; long live the photo-essay" with the goal of creating a collaborative rapid-prototype publication. The workshop brought together contemporary art photographers, photo journalists and anthropologists who were challenged ahead of the workshop to bring photo-essays in progress. Over an afternoon, supplies were given, scissors were used, dialogue occurred, and 36 hours later a zine was produced collaboratively. It is these types of multimodal experiments that emphasize process and collaboration that bode well for photography in anthropology. The goal being "To disrupt, to re-define, and to work within and beyond the photographic frame" (Ethnographic Terminalia 2017).

We also look at projects like Critical Visions by Stephanie N. Sadre-Orafai and her students at the University of Cincinnati who continually publish multimodal works in novel collaborative ways. We also appreciate the ethnographic work of Brent Luvaas on fashion blogging and street style for multimodal inspiration. In this project, Luvaas sees the rise of amateur fashion photographers as a means of pushing back against dominant modes of interpretation by positioning street photographers as the experts and amateur ethnographers. He also situates these practices as a means to question the democratization of access, authority, class positionality, and meaning (Luvaas 2017). His work may seem similar to something like the social media project "Humans of New York" in all of its many iterations, but it is not. "Humans of New York" sucks. Sure the photographs are beautiful and

Figure 3.12 "The photo-essay is dead; long live the photo-essay"
Source: Ethnographic Terminalia. Cover was designed by Sam Gould (Beyond Repair, MN)

the brief stories are compelling in their limited way, but there are no contextual questions that strive for larger interpretive meaning. There is no discussion of collaboration. The project is just something to maybe make you feel good. Cool, we guess? What multimodality really does is break down and shatter any idea that there is a special difference between what anthropologists and other people do. Why would posting photos be anthropological when everyone is doing the same thing? Rather, it is the accentuation of everything but the photo itself that speaks to a multimodal and anthropological approach. Our favorite exemplar for this type of work are the blurred photographs taken by Jason DeLeon's collaborators. The photos are produced by his interlocutors, they are valued as ethnographic by the anthropologist, and the context provided for them interrogates structural violence (De León and Wells 2015).

Here is a fun photo elicitation project to conduct with your students. We use this to get students to think critically about representations of Baltimore where we teach using Harper's essay on photo elicitation. It's also fun for them to interrogate family and friends and create uncomfortable conversations as fledgling anthropologists. After all, that's what we do best, right? Simply replace "Baltimore" with wherever you may be in the world.

Classroom Exercises

1. Read the article "Talking about pictures, a case for photo elicitation" by Doug Harper (link: www.nyu.edu/classes/bkg/methods/harper.pdf). Answer the following reading questions about the reading:

    a. What is the definition of photo elicitation?
    b. When and how was photo elicitation first used as a method?
    c. Identify and describe the four areas where photo elicitation has been concentrated.
    d. How does Harper discuss the notions of "brake the frame" and "building a bridge."

2. Answer the following interview questions yourself:

    a. What do you think of the City of Baltimore?
    b. What do you think people outside of the city think about Baltimore? Regionally? Nationally?
    c. What do you think are the biggest problems facing Baltimore?
    d. What are the reasons Baltimore faces various problems like these?

3. Review the Wide Angle Youth Media website in order to understand their history, mission, and programming (http://wideanglemedia.org/). Review the book *This Is Baltimore* and complete the following tasks:

    a. Pick 20 images that you want to emphasize in your interview to elicit reactions from your interview collaborator.
    b. Pick ten of those images to write your own personal reflection on each image.

4. Conduct an interview with a collaborator… a family member, friend, or close associate. Explain the assignment. Explain the method of photo elicitation. Discuss the group Wide Angle Youth Media. Then ask the following questions and document their responses verbatim as much as possible or by paraphrasing (if you record them you must transcribe them for the assignment and not turn in a digital or video recording):

    a. What do you think of the City of Baltimore?
    b. What do you think people outside of the city think about Baltimore? Regionally? Nationally?
    c. What do you think are the biggest problems facing Baltimore?
    d. What are the reasons Baltimore faces various problems like these?
    e. Open the *This Is Baltimore* book. Have your collaborator go through the book, feel free to discuss the book, Baltimore, or whatever may come up. *This portion of the method should be free-flowing but do not identify the pictures that you have selected.*

Have them identify ten pictures that they like, dislike, or react to. Give them time to do so. Feel free to leave them to do this on their own and come back to you, but you may be able to elicit reactions more if you stay. Identify each of the ten pictures that they chose by title/page number and detail their reaction to each one.

(End the conversation by thanking them for the interview.)

5 Write a brief reflection essay of a few paragraphs on the entire process with the following elements. Compare the answers to questions a–d between yourself and your collaborator. Compare the photos you selected and your reactions to them with those of your collaborator. Does the book change or add to you and your collaborator's perception of Baltimore? Were you surprised by any reaction during the elicitation process? Using Harper's article, did you or your collaborator "break the frame" in your elicitation when it comes to Baltimore and its population? Did the images "become a bridge" for communication between you and your collaborator?

References

Becker, H.S. (1974). Photography and sociology. *Studies in Visual Communication, 1* (1), 3–26. https://repository.upenn.edu/svc/vol1/iss1/3.

Chan, S. (2008). Revisiting the other half of Jacob Riis. *New York Times*. https://archive.nytimes.com/cityroom.blogs.nytimes.com/2008/02/28/revisiting-the-other-half-of-jacob-riis/.

Collier, J. Jr. (1957). Photography in anthropology: A report on two experiments. *American Anthropologist*, 59(5), 843–859.

Curtis, E. (1999). *Edward S. Curtis's The North American Indian photographic images* [Photograph]. Library of Congress. https://lccn.loc.gov/2003557114.

De León, J., & Wells, M. (2015). *The land of open graves: Living and dying on the migrant trail* (1st edn). University of California Press. www.jstor.org/stable/10.1525/j.ctv1xxvch.

Durington, M. (2007). The ethnographic semiotics of a suburban moral panic. *Critical Arts*, 21(2), 261–275. DOI: doi:10.1080/02560040701810040.

Durington, M. and Demyan, N. (2012). Bourgois, Philippe and Schonberg, Jeff. *Righteous Dopefiend*. Berkeley: University of California Press, 2009. *North American Dialogue*, 15, 60–63. https://doi.org/10.1111/j.1556-4819.2012.01054.x.

Edwards, E. (ed.) (1994). *Anthropology and photography, 1860–1920*. Yale University Press.

Evans, B. & Glass, A. (eds) (2014) *Return to the land of the head hunters: Edward S. Curtis, the Kwakwaka'wakw, and the making of modern cinema*. University of Washington Press.

Fabian, J. (2014). Front matter. In *Time and the other: How anthropology makes its object*. Columbia University Press, pp. i–iv. www.jstor.org/stable/10.7312/fabi16926.1.

Favero, P. (2017). Tainted frictions: A visual essay. *American Anthropologist*, 119(2), 361–364.
Gidley, M. (2006). The making of Edward S. Curtis's *The North American Indian*. *The Princeton University Library Chronicle*, 67(2), 314–329. https://doi.org/10.25290/prinunivlibrchro.67.2.0314.
Glass, A. (2009). A cannibal in the archive: Performance, materiality, and (in)visibility in unpublished Edward Curtis photographs of the Kwakwaka'wakw Hamat'sa. *Visual Anthropology Review*, 25, 128–149. https://doi.org/10.1111/j.1548-7458.2009.01038.x.
Golub, A. (2018). Where the whacky Franz Boas pictures come from. *Addendum*, January. https://anthrodendum.org/2018/01/12/where-the-crazy-franz-boas-pictures-come-from/.
Greenfield, P. (2018). National Geographic: For decades, our coverage was racist. *The Guardian*. www.theguardian.com/world/2018/mar/13/national-geographic-magazine-coverage-racist.
Greenwood, D.J., & Levin, M. (1998). Action research, science, and co-optation of social research. *Studies in Cultures, Organizations and Societies*, 4, 237–261.
Gross, L. (1980). Sol Worth and the study of visual communications. *Study of Visual Communications*, 6(3), 2–19. https://repository.upenn.edu/svc/vol6/iss3/2.
Gubrium, A., Harper, K., & Otañez, M. (eds) (2015). *Participatory visual and digital research in action* (1st edn). Routledge.
Harper, D. (2002). Talking about pictures: A case for photo elicitation. *Visual Studies*, 17(1), 13–26. http://dx.doi.org/10.1080/14725860220137345.
Harper, K., Sands, C., Angarita, D., Totman, M.et al. (2017). Food justice youth development: Using Photovoice to study urban school food systems. Local Environment, 22(7), 1–18.
Harper, K., Steger, T., & Filcak, R. (2009) Environmental justice and Roma communities in Central and Eastern Europe. *Environmental Policy and Governance*, 19(4), 251–268.
Ivins, W. (1969) *Prints and visual communication*. MIT Press.
Jacknis, I. (1984). Franz Boas and photography. *Visual Studies in Communication*, 10 (1), 2–60. https://repository.upenn.edu/svc/vol10/iss1/2.
Kedia, S., & van Willigen, J. (eds) (2005). *Applied anthropology: Domains of application*. Praeger.
Lutz, C. and Collins, J. (1993). *Reading National Geographic*. University of Chicago Press.
Luvaas, B. (2017). Ethnography and street photography. *Anthropology News*, 58: e325–e332. https://doi.org/10.1111/AN.393
Maxwell, A. (2013). Modern anthropology and the problem of the racial type: The photographs of Franz Boas. *Visual Communication*, 12(1), 123–142. https://doi.org/10.1177/1470357212462782.
Pinney, C. (2011). *Photography and anthropology*. University of Chicago Press.
Rotha, P. (1980). Nanook and the North. *Visual Studies in Communication*, 6(2), 33–60. https://repository.upenn.edu/svc/vol6/iss2/4.
Ruby, J. (1980). Introduction: A reevaluation of Robert J. Flaherty, photographer and filmmaker. *Visual Studies in Communication*, 6(2), 2–4. https://repository.upenn.edu/svc/vol6/iss2/2.
Ruby, J. (ed.) (1982). *A crack in the mirror: Reflexive perspectives in anthropology*. University of Pennsylvania Press.

Ruby, J. (1991). Speaking for, speaking about, speaking with, or speaking alongside: An anthropological and documentary dilemma. *Visual Anthropology Review*, 7, 50–67. https://doi.org/10.1525/var.1991.7.2.50.

Ruby, J. (2000). *Picturing culture: Explorations of film and anthropology*. University of Chicago Press.

Sands, C., Harper, K., Reed, L.E., & Shar, M. (2009). A photovoice participatory evaluation of a school gardening program through the eyes of fifth graders. *Practicing Anthropology*, 31(4), 15–20.

Shankar, A. (2016). Auteurship and image-making: A (gentle) critique of the photovoice method. *Visual Anthropology Review*, 32, 157–166. https://doi.org/10.1111/var.12107.

Wang, C., & Burris, M.A. (1997). Photovoice: Concept, methodology, and use for participatory needs assessment. *Health Education & Behavior*, 24(3), 369–387. DOI: doi:10.1177/109019819702400309.

4 Mapping the Community

Asset mapping has long been a tool in community research, but the spread of freely available, relatively low-tech walking tour and GIS applications allows anthropologists and their interlocutors to represent their community, its strengths and its problems, not only for people in the community, but for other visitors, researchers, and even for grantors. This chapter describes multimedia methods for asset mapping and outlines advantages for people in the community and for anthropologists in terms of data and community empowerment.

Maps as a Colonial Tool

Maps have always been a tool of power – of the military, of the state, of the powerful against the powerless. Maps (along with things like hedges) were important technologies in the divestiture of peasants from the Commons during the Enclosure period (Blomley 2007). And they were deployed by colonial powers throughout the 18th and 19th centuries to demarcate and order people, territory, and ethnicity; later they become the basis for independence from those same colonial powers. They are powerful technologies for domination and, as Anderson writes, "profoundly shaped the way in which the colonial state imagined its dominion – the nature of the human beings it ruled, the geography of its domain, and the legitimacy of its ancestry" (Anderson 2016: 161). The power of the map follows places into the post-colonial era, with the ethnic and linguistic boundaries set by the British contributing to recent political strife (among other, more proximate, causes) (MacArthur 2016). Many of these maps have proved both ruinous and long-lasting; Dean Rusk and Charles Bonesteel divided the Korean peninsula with a sweep of the pen, initiating a painful division which has persisted for almost 80 years:

> Without particular knowledge of Korea or even a precise map, Rusk and Bonesteel sliced it like a birthday cake, leaving the capital in the south and pushing in the knife a tad further north than they actually

DOI: 10.4324/9781003330851-5

believed would be acceptable to the Soviets. In the event, the Soviets made no objections and halted at the agreed upon line.

(Thomas 2009: 5)

Divisive and exclusionary, many of the problems today are the result of colonial mapping, as a form of knowledge that both "opens" territories to colonial expropriation while closing peoples into proscribed geographies.

Within cities, maps have played a similar role. In the hands of government officials, planners, developers, public health advocates, and real estate agents, maps have been technologies to parse populations, to acquire land, and to convert use value into exchange value. In Baltimore, "Residential security maps" that were the product of a partnership between government and the real estate industry resulted in "redlining," the mapping of investment "risk" which happened to coincide precisely with the mapping of non-white populations.

That redlining map, as Lawrence Brown has conclusively demonstrated, persists today in all of the city's inequalities – from housing to education and health care. Everything follows the "Black Butterfly" and the "White L": the demarcations laid down in the 1930s (Brown 2021).

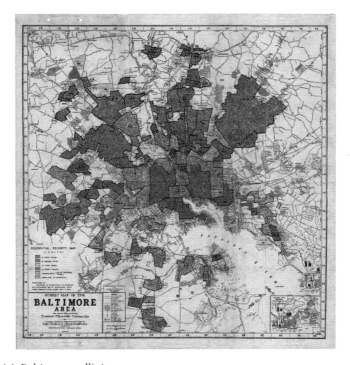

Figure 4.1 Baltimore redlining map

The role of anthropology in these powerful mappings has been very often complicit – although occasionally resistant. Some of the earliest applications included Clark Wissler's "culture area" maps of Native Americans, a method of "spatializing" culture in a way that afforded anthropologists the power to make panoptic proclamations about different Native American groups and their relationships to each other – never mind that these were inaccurate (Kroeber 1931; Willmott 2021). By the 1960s, the complicity of the approach with government oppression was even more glaring, and when Eric Wolf wrote that "Names thus become things, and things marked with an x can become targets of war," he assuredly had anthropologists in mind who had "mapped" Southeast Asian ethnic groups (Wolf 1982: 7). Marcel Griaule, certainly, thought of the map as an instrument in a "war" for ethnographic knowledge of the Dogon: "The simple fact of drawing up a map could give an overview and initial mastery of the culture inscribed on the land" (Clifford 1988: 69).

More recent work in anthropology has looked to more emancipatory possibilities in participatory mapping as a tool of resistance against dominant power. As a method, participatory mapping can be used to elucidate social networks, folks models and cosmologies, or geographies; anthropologists have generally engaged in this last one. Here, anthropologists and others work with indigenous and marginalized groups to map resources, territories, and spatial practice with the goal of helping people exert their claims on states and other powerful agents. Methodologically, many of the same tools used in ethnographic research pertain here: interviews, transect walks, asset maps. These can illuminate spatial knowledge that was heretofore completely invisible to outsiders. In the "Digital Matatus" project, Nairobi students mapped the routes of informal minibuses (matatus) over a period of months using their own knowledge and through interviews with other residents. Paper maps of the routes were then distributed; later, apps of the routes were developed that allow people to plan their transit around matatus and other forms of transportation. Goals of the project included more effective planning and, in general, greater transportation equity for Nairobi residents. At the same time, as Klopp and Cavoli (2019) caution, mapping projects like Digital Mataus can also enable the state to undermine independent transit through exercising panoptic control over routes. Nevertheless, the authors conclude that participatory mapping projects like this "will become even more important as urban planners move away from a focus on achieving large transport projects towards more integrated multi-modal systems that generate access and equity" (Klopp and Cavoli 2019: 672). There are also many mapping projects that enlist indigenous communities in creating maps of their territory and resource use, the goal of which is to make claims against the state or other extractivist agents trying to exploit the community.

When we look at the maps that we've made with people in communities, we've realized the potential for them to be re-appropriated into the commodified city. This process is already readily evident in Baltimore, where historic, industrial structures have been re-purposed and appropriated into Baltimore's "Eds, Beds and Meds" development strategy. For example, Camden Yards, the home of the Baltimore Orioles baseball team, is built around older structures from the B&O Railroad, including Camden Station, which forms part of the eastern border to the stadium. While this might be an example of "adaptive re-use," it is also the obfuscation of that history. Ingram (2015: 319) writes:

> A key aspect of this veiling process has been the repossession and incorporation of elements of Baltimore's history into the revitalized body of the city. The cobbled streets of Fells Point, the exposed steel girders at Harborplace Market, and the B&O Warehouse monolith at Oriole Park at Camden Yards conspire to create the sense that the consumer's experience of these places is the experience of the real Baltimore. These historical signifiers, long indicators of post-industrial ruin, are now integral elements in nearly all new development, recycling the signifiers of an ongoing poverty as integral elements of the city's consumer spectacle.

Camden Station was the site of especially bloody labor struggles, including the Baltimore rail strike of 1877, which ended with US troops firing into a crowd of protestors at the behest of railroad owners.

When we add historical or noteworthy sites to our maps – however participatory that process might be – how easy is it for these to be re-appropriated into the gentrified, tourist city? Our storymap collaboration with people in Sharp Leadenhall is detailed below, and we are happy with the way that the work has enabled the articulation of local voices, but the gentrification of the neighborhood has continued. In this context, critical evocations of place can simply be reabsorbed as "cultural value" providing highly reified "history" and "texture" to revanchist developers commodifying community.

Rather than contest images of the city as a "growth machine" as in Figure 4.2 – as about development and profit – re-appropriations can simply turn these maps into places of interest for the tourist and sources of value for the developer.

Participatory mapping can be one part of a multimodal anthropology, but – as with all of the media and media platforms we consider here – it must be accompanied by other media that might help mitigate against its appropriation. As Bryan (2011: 49) concludes of participatory mapping projects with indigenous peoples:

> As a social practice, mapping is contingent and fleeting. Having a map no more equates with the implementation of neoliberal reforms than it does with the protection of indigenous rights. Instead their production and use helps enframe a set of political possibilities, distinguishing peoples' practical knowledge of a socio-spatial order writ in terms of colonialism, dispossession and inequality from a new order configured in terms of law and property.

82 *Mapping the Community*

Figure 4.2 The growth machine in South Baltimore

Participatory mapping opens up possibilities as well as hazards – in other words, the multimodal "mangle of practice," to re-purpose the work of Andrew Pickering (1995). The multimodal "mangle" acknowledges ethnographic fieldwork as the product of multiple agents. Moreover, those agents are variously embedded in power structures that connect and reconnect to each other in a stochastic dance that will demand our continued vigilance.

Storymapping

Poppleton:
Over the last 20 years, the University of Maryland Medical Center (UMMC) has been expanding into West Baltimore – the mirror image of Johns Hopkins Hospital in East Baltimore. This has included luxury apartments in working-class neighborhoods in West Baltimore through a government-brokered deal with a private developer – La Cité – that involved using eminent domain to clear out existing homeowners. In Baltimore, eminent domain has been a weapon for the forceful removal of working-class, largely African Americans residents from their communities for decades, and the "fair" value people receive for the properties rarely allows them to buy homes in "better" neighborhoods. These payments, of course, do little to replace communities that have been destroyed (Gomez 2015). When people objected to their homes being taken, the City dug in, moving to evict Poppleton's residents. But Poppleton residents, under the leadership of long-time resident Sonia Eaddy, began organizing resistance against the development scheme (Snowden and Soderberg 2021).

Eventually, Nicole King, faculty in the American Studies Department at the nearby University of Maryland Baltimore County, taught a class featuring the campaign, and King and her students created a variety of media to document the history of the neighborhood, and the importance of Poppleton to the community. They worked with Poppleton residents to create brochures, and invited City officials to tour the neighborhood. One of the outcomes of these efforts was a storymap, a multimedia narrative of place.

In "A place called Poppleton storymap," King and her students combined interviews, videos, text, and photographs, all pegged to significant locations in Poppleton, including the embattled Sarah Anne Street alley homes. Finally, in July of 2022, the City relented, and agreed to modify their development scheme to preserve Poppleton. The battle continues over other portions of the neighborhood and, more broadly, to the question of what constitutes equitable development in Baltimore.

In the "city as growth machine" model of development, places are only important to the extent they generate value (Logan and Molotch 1987). Good "cultural institutions" increase real estate values, and cities woo private developers in order to generate that value. Lost here are the social lives and practices of communities, which are all but rendered invisible in the process. For example, many of the neighborhoods in Baltimore where we've worked have been extremely stable, filled with long-term residents, but renters, rather than homeowners. The social and cultural investments they've made in their communities are effaced in policies that privilege homeowners over renters, and development over stability. By highlighting place and narrating its meaning, storymaps reveal the richness of community that is effaced in the commodification of neighborhoods.

Storymaps have become nearly synonymous with a particular software package: esri's ArcGIS, a well-established Geographic Information Systems software that allows users to map multiple "layers" on top of each other. ArcGIS StoryMap allows maps and other media to be narrated together into a combination of a "story" with illustrative, digital data. The result has become a fixture of the digital humanities, and versions of ArcGIS StoryMaps feature in countless online news and magazine stories (Howland et al. 2020). These have allowed for effective combinations of historical research, ethnographic data, multimedia, and mapping. At the same time, ArcGIS StoryMap is not a free application, and, while it is certainly easier for people to learn than other GIS tools, there are nevertheless several obstacles to communities that might want to use it for their own self-representation. We have explored several other applications (in addition to ArcGIS) with the ultimate goal of accessibility and collaboration – a multimodal ethos that we recognize is both evolving and elusive. The examples below discuss some of our work on storymaps, and the contexts in which they've been used.

Case Study #1: Suffrage Map

We were approached in 2018 by the National Park Service to work on a project that would mark the 100th anniversary of the 19th Amendment guaranteeing women's suffrage. The Park Service was also interested in bringing together various stakeholder communities, among them park rangers, park visitors, archivists, database managers, women's studies scholars and students. We proposed a network map (called a sociograph) overlaid on top of a geographical map of the United States, showing correspondence between suffrage activists (see Figure 4.3).

The hope for this project was to use correspondence networks to present an alternative narrative of suffrage – one that might cut across some of the fractious divisions the movement gradually splintered into (e.g., the National Woman Suffrage Association versus the American Woman Suffrage Association), racial divisions, and political battles. Here, it joined other research in the digital humanities that has applied social network analysis to suffrage and other movements in order to evoke alternative histories (Rosenthal et al. 1985; Elford 2016). In particular, we hoped to use the power of correspondence networks to join local place to national movements, noting that the battle for suffrage was at once a national movement with instantly recognizable figures such as Elizabeth Cady Stanton, but that it was also a resolutely local movement, with chapters in cities and small towns across the United States, including African American, Asian American, and LatinX activists.

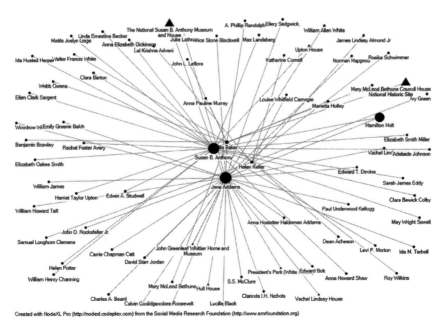

Figure 4.3 Suffrage nodes

Mapping the Community 85

We presented our ideas in a workshop with many stakeholders, alongside our students and GIS specialists from our university. One of the changes from that workshop was an emphasis on places that people could visit: NPS sites, house museums, monuments. Not only the acknowledgment that suffrage activists were part of a national movement, but that this movement was localized in a place, with cities, countries, and states presenting different topologies of political oppression and emancipatory possibilities (Ewald 2009).

Of the storymapping applications that we introduced in the workshop, only one (esri's ArcGIS) had been officially employed by the National Park Service, so this was the default package for our project. Using it, we have mapped correspondence (see Figure 4.4) linking thousands of people, among them suffrage activists, journalists, politicians, labor organizers, abolitionists, and many others, demonstrating that the movement for women's suffrage bears many similarities to the emphasis on "affinity" in New Social Movements.

The initial work for this map was archival, with researchers looking to finding aids and vertical files of correspondence. We knew from the outset, though, that many of these correspondence networks would be effectively invisible. The archive, after all, presupposes selection (whose records are kept?), labor (whose records are processed?), and dissemination (whose records are available? Is there a finding aid?). In the history of women's suffrage, these over-emphasize certain activities at the expense of others, and those "others" include many non-white people, whose own archives and correspondence may sit in the closet of a church office rather than in the archives of a research library – but are no less important for all that (Schwartz and Cook 2002). Since 2020, however,

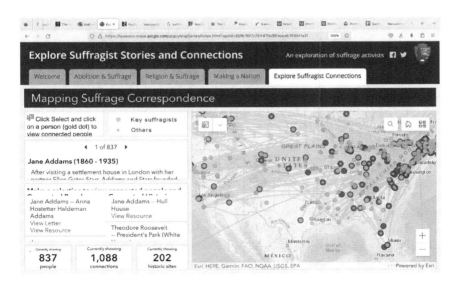

Figure 4.4 Suffrage map screenshot

86 *Mapping the Community*

we have been crowdsourcing data from people who might have more of a local knowledge of suffrage activism and who could be a source of more diverse, more nuanced suffrage networks that are oftentimes passed over in larger histories of the movement (Standish et al. 2020). Through interviews, and through work with other stakeholders, we're expanding this research into a complex network of people and place.

Although much of this work took place over the course of the pandemic, we nevertheless held an online event in August of 2020 introducing the map – on the 100-year anniversary of the 19th Amendment. Speakers included prominent women in Baltimore, NPS staff, and students who had worked with us on the project.

Case Study #2: Greenmount West

In early 2019, we joined a number of community groups at a workshop at the Baltimore Museum of Art regarding the Greenmount West neighborhood in Baltimore. As both a neighborhood with a long African American history and as the center of recent real estate development around the arts, Greenmount West is a place where long-time, largely African American residents have been forced out of their homes by rampant gentrification (Rich 2019; Collins and Durington 2020). A few months later, we partnered with the Greenmount West Community Center and its Director, Candace Everette, in order to work with children at the Center to produce a storymap of their neighborhood. This started with asset mapping and transect walks, which revealed favorite places, stories, murals, and community meeting places. We co-produced community maps, and then toured them again with recording equipment. The children filmed each other narrating the important places in their lives, and we worked together to analyze and edit the recordings.

Noting that ArcGIS was too technical for our co-authors, we opted to use the "Knight Lab" Storymap, a free, web-based application that allows for photographs and for embedded media. The storymap was also the basis for a walking tour on the izi.travel platform. The results were published online, and an accompanying article co-authored by everyone involved was published several months later (Collins and Durington 2020) (see Figure 4.5).

At the end of the summer of 2019, we had finished the StoryMap, which we included in an exhibit we installed at The Peale, a "community museum" that features place-based storytelling and Baltimore artists and performers. Running on an old iMac computer, the storymap stood next to maps the children had made, and photos they had taken of their community. Finally, the children and the Greenmount West Community Center performed dance and spoken word at the Baltimore Museum of Art, an event that included their thoughts on the gentrification of their community.

Mapping the Community 87

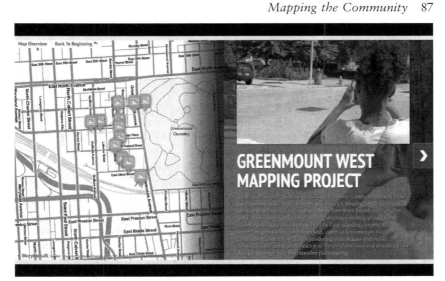

Figure 4.5 Greenmount West, izi.travel screenshot

Case Study #3: Walking Tours – Sharp Leadenhall Project

In 2016, we were funded by the MuseWeb Foundation to work with two community groups on a digital walking tour in South Baltimore's Sharp Leadenhall neighborhood. Sharp Leadenhall has a long history: it is the oldest African American neighborhood in Baltimore, dating back to the late 18th century. Frederick Douglass delivered a speech at the corner of West Hill and Sharp Streets under a massive tree – now referred to as the "Frederick Douglass Tree" – and generations of famous African American residents of Baltimore grew up there. However, the neighborhood has been threatened repeatedly over the course of the last two centuries by the city's racist policies. In the late 1960s, the city planned to build an interstate through Baltimore's east side, across the Inner Harbor and through Sharp Leadenhall. By the time the coalition of activists (Movement Against Destruction) had gathered enough strength to defeat the highway, a number of homes in Sharp Leadenhall had already been condemned to make way for the project, forcing many of the neighborhood's African American renters to move (Paull 2022). A few years later, the area was at the epicenter of the mayor's "dollar home" scheme to develop South Baltimore by selling homes cheaply to people who could verify they had the monetary resources to rehabilitate the properties – again to the disadvantage of Sharp Leadenhall's African American renters. As gentrification squeezed the neighborhood from the east and Baltimore's stadium complex from the west (on land that used to be Sharp Leadenhall), Sharp Leadenhall continued to shrink (Durington et al. 2009).

We had worked with members of the Sharp Leadenhall community for years to document these changes and to help them tell their story of an African American neighborhood under pressure from gentrification. Now, with money from MuseWeb, we were able to engage Wide Angle Youth Media, a Baltimore non-profit working with young people to produce multimedia, and work with Betty Bland-Thomas, a Sharp Leadenhall community activist and the President of the South Baltimore Partnership, in order to build a walking tour of the neighborhood. Additional input for the tour came from Thomas Gillard, a former resident of the community who led tours of his childhood neighborhood with us during our "Anthropology by the Wire" project. Wide Angle youth worked on editing interviews and on audio narration for the tour.

One of the most interesting aspects of the Sharp Leadenhall project, however, was the platform itself. Izi.travel is a website and mobile app that hosts walking tours in hundreds of cities across the world. It began as a platform for museum tours, but began to shift over to walking tours a few months before we used it in 2016. The platform uses OpenStreetMap and geolocation to link multimedia content to places. Creators set the circumference of a geolocated "circle" around the content, and when people touring the site intersect with those boundaries, the platform triggers the multimedia.

The 20-stop tour has been cross-posted across many websites, and has been utilized to help reinforce the historic qualities of the neighborhood, even as development and gentrification have continued to chip away at the core of long-time residents. We have assigned this tour dozens of times in classes, and used it as a prompt to help others think about their own Baltimore tours. One of our community partners – Temple X in northwest Baltimore – used the platform for its own tour of their Ashburton neighborhood, one featuring the children in the neighborhood and designed to ameliorate some of the effects of being shut in their homes during the pandemic (Broderick 2020).

Content on the izi.travel site has continued to evolve. Universities, non-profits, and others have posted hundreds of walking tours of Baltimore highlighting historic and contemporary features of place. We have utilized it for classes documenting "hostile design," environmental pollution and embattled public spaces. In 2017, we received some money from Towson University's Office of Civic Engagement to support students at Ben Franklin High School in Curtis Bay, a working class neighborhood in South Baltimore, to make a walking tour highlighting environmental justice themes in their community, a neighborhood that has the worst toxic air pollution of any in the state (Wheeler 2012). The tour was a (small) part of coordinated activities undertaken by Free Your Voice, a community-activist group founded by neighborhood high school students and devoted to combating the neighborhood's air pollution (Fabricant 2023). These activities included demonstrations and city council hearings, alongside writing, organizing, performance, and other media dramatizing the plight of neighborhood residents and the culpability of industries in polluting Curtis Bay.

As with other tools and platforms we discuss in this book, izi.travel raises some ethical questions. First, it is a for-profit venture. While creators might create tours and upload content for free to the site, the mobile app prompts you to subscribe to a plan for the service – although you can defer this step until later. Second, the fate of these media is unclear. Already, we note that the tour has been cross-posted on other GPS tour sites – and it's unclear how these are related to izi.travel itself. Nevertheless, the tour has never been appropriated into a context that would change its meaning – it's still about the threats of gentrification to a historically rich and resilient African American neighborhood in Baltimore. Moreover, its cross-posting on different platforms means that more people have an opportunity to see the content. You don't actually need to walk this tour to see the content; it's all visible from the izi.travel website (for free). Still, all of the usual questions about access still pertain, in terms of who can see it, and under what circumstances.

Conclusion

Go to "Google Maps" and search for Greenmount West. Aside from churches and schools, the most prominent "pin" on the map belongs to a brewpub, a new business located in a former factory space and a sign of gentrification. A few blocks from Baltimore's train station, it signals the changing population of Greenmount West and underscores the dominance of business interests in maps produced by corporations. Our map-making with youth in the neighborhood is invisible – at least on this platform. Realistically, as anthropologists partnering with community groups, we have little chance of changing those maps – the maps created by government, real estate, and corporations to pathologize, vilify, commodify, gentrify. Yet none of the projects we've outlined here ends with the production of a map; all are one step in larger, multimodal projects that connect media and social action with place-making. Finally, the walking tours we've helped to produce add walking itself as a form of critique, one that sets one "node" in a constellation of knowledge about self, other, and place (Ingold 2010).

Maps, then, may fit into a panoply of different multimodal productions – one of several outcomes for an anthropological project. None of the foregoing examples stood alone; they accompanied other media, performance, exhibits. Like other multimodal platforms, maps are meant to (literally) connect us to something else – to an interview, a gallery show, a social movement. So, despite the continuing dominance of maps that naturalize inequality and obscure resistance, the mapping here is one piece in larger projects that connect to stakeholders and policymakers in ways that might make a difference.

Despite the importance of embedding maps in other multimodal strategies, there are nevertheless critical and even utopian possibilities in these maps. Confronted by "official" discourses that erase African American histories from putatively "white" parts of Rochester, New York, Mariner develops a walking tour of the city that focuses on absences and on suppressed pasts:

> My walking tour is critically fabulated not because the points of interest that we'll visit are fictional – they all exist – but because the walking tour itself, the racialized discursive and geographical frame I'm using to hold these spaces in dialogue and in tension, is a speculative attempt to illuminate the ways in which physical and geographic space can become an archive for social exclusion and historical erasure.
>
> (Mariner 2022: 13)

Highlighting sites of erasure – the empty lots, suppressed histories – Mariner sketches a vision of Rochester where African American space has been effaced by whiteness. Yet, in doing so, Mariner simultaneously raises the possibility of a future where Rochester acknowledges its African American history and present: "To call attention to stark patterns of racial erasure in Rochester is to build upon a rich tradition of Black resistance, and toward a fertile future for Black placemaking" (Mariner 2022: 15).

Storymaps and walking tours may not possess the force to directly contest, say, the redlining that continues (under different rationales) in places like Baltimore, but they do conjure other possibilities. They are, in other words, a form of world-making, an evocation of an "otherwise" composed of "latent possibilities and potentialities held within a situation or formation; possibilities we might only glimpse obliquely, which are 'prefigured but not formed,' yet that 'hold and open' an otherwise as liberatory transformation" (Meek and Morales Fontanilla 2022: 2). Not a rupture with the hegemony of official maps, but what Agamben (1998) calls "tiny displacements." When people trace another's path through a community, glimpses of other sources of meaning and value are visible through the overdetermined patina of capital and commodification. These places pegged to maps and accompanied by photos and interviews are the "not-yet" for more equitable place-making. "Not-yet" is a reference to the work of Ernst Bloch, who saw utopia in everyday acts and texts. Collaborating with members of the community to make maps is not just the evocation of other possibilities, it shows a will.

Classroom Exercise

Using Knight Lab's free storymapping platform, map the "daily round" of someone close to you. Include pictures and textual description. What are your interpretations?

What is a daily round? Definition: the usual activities of one's day. This may be interpreted in a number of ways – feel free to experiment.

References

Agamben, G. (1998). *Homo sacer: Sovereign power and bare life.* Stanford University Press.

Anderson, B.R. (2016). *Imagined communities: Reflections on the origin and spread of nationalism* (rev. edn). Verso.

Blomley, N. (2007). Making private property. *Rural History,* 18(1), 1–21.

Broderick, K. (2020). Kids create app to help learn historical significance of Baltimore area. *WMAR News,* August 18. www.wmar2news.com/news/region/baltimore-city/kids-create-app-to-help-learn-historical-significance-of-baltimore-area.

Brown, L. (2021). *The black butterfly.* Johns Hopkins University Press.

Bryan, J. (2011). Walking the line: Participatory mapping, indigenous rights, and neoliberalism. *Geoforum,* 42(1), 40–50. https://doi.org/10.1016/j.geoforum.2010.09.001.

Clifford, J. (1988). *The predicament of culture: Twentieth-century ethnography, literature, and art.* Harvard University Press. https://doi.org/10.2307/j.ctvjf9x0h.

Collins, S.G., & Durington, M.S. (2020). The case for letting anthropology be quarantines: COVID and the end of ethnographic presence. *Entanglements,* 3(2), 92–96.

Durington, M., Maddox, C., Ruhf, A., Gass, S., & Schwermer, J. (2009). Civic engagement and gentrification issues in metropolitan Baltimore. *Metropolitan Studies,* 20(1), 101–114.

Elford, J.S. (2016). Recovering women's history with network analysis. *Journal of Modern Periodical Studies,* 6(2), 191–213.

Ewald, A.C. (2009). *The way we vote: The local dimension of American suffrage.* Vanderbilt University Press.

Fabricant, N. (2023). *Fighting to breathe.* University of California Press.

Gomez, M. (2015). *Race, class, power and organizing in East Baltimore.* Lexington Books.

Howland, M.D., Liss, B., Levy, T.E., & Najjar, M. (2020). Integrating digital datasets into public engagement through ArcGIS. *Advances in Archaeological Oractice,* 8(4), 351–360.

Ingold, T. (2010). Ways of mind-walking: reading, writing, painting. *Visual Studies,* 25(1), 15–23.

Ingram, C. (2015). Building between past and future: Nostalgia, historical materialism and the architecture of memory in Baltimore's Inner Harbor. *Philosophy & Social Criticism,* 41(3), 317–333. https://doi.org/10.1177/0191453714556690.

Klopp, J.M. & Cavoli, C. (2019) Mapping minibuses in Maputo and Nairobi: Engaging paratransit in transportation planning in African cities. *Transport Reviews,* 39(5), 657–676. DOI: doi:10.1080/01441647.2019.1598513.

Kroeber, A.L. (1931). The culture-area and age-area concepts of Clark Wissler. In S.A. Rice (ed.), *Methods in social sciences.* University of Chicago Press, pp. 248–265.

Logan, J.R., & Molotch, H.L. (1987). *Urban fortunes: The political economy of place.* University of California Press.

MacArthur, J. (2016). *Cartographies and the political imagination.* Ohio University Press.

Mariner, K.A. (2022). Where are all the Black people at? *Transforming Anthropology,* 30(1), 3–19.

Meek, L.A., & Morales Fontanilla, J.A. (2022). Otherwise. *Feminist Anthropology,* 3(2), 274–283.

Paull, E.E. (2022). *Stop the road.* Boyle & Dalton.

Pickering, A. (1995). *The mangle of practice: Time, agency, and science.* University of Chicago Press.

Rich, M.A. (2019) "Artists are a tool for gentrification": Maintaining artists and creative production in arts districts. *International Journal of Cultural Policy*, 25 (6), 727–742,

Rosenthal, N., & Fingrutd, M., Ethier, M., Karant, R., & McDonald, D. (1985). Social movements and network analysis: A case study of nineteenth-century women's reform in New York State. *American Journal of Sociology*, 90(5), 1022–1054.

Schwartz, J.M., & Cook, T. (2002). Archives, records, and power: The making of modern memory. *Archival Science*, 2, 1–19.

Snowden, L., & Soderberg, B. (2021). "West Baltimore Ruins" preserves the memory of neglected neighborhoods before they're lost to gentrification. *The Real News Network.* https://therealnews.com/west-baltimore-ruins-preserves-the-memory-of-neglected-neighborhoods-before-theyre-lost-to-gentrification.

Standish, J., Andersen, C.V., Antoine, S., Fitch, F., & Kinoti, K. (2020). In place to make change: NC2020 and the commemoration of women's suffrage. *Southern Cultures*, 26(3), 156–171.

Thomas, J.A. (2009). The exquisite corpses of nature and history. *The Asia-Pacific Journal*, 7(43), 1–16.

Wheeler, T. (2012). Study says Curtis Bay, Brooklyn among MD's most polluted areas. *Baltimore Sun*, March 15. www.baltimoresun.com/news/environment/bal-study-says-curtis-bay-brooklyn-among-mds-most-polluted-areas-20120315-story.html.

Willmott, C. (2021). Decolonizing the museum to reclaim and revitalize the Anishinaabe strap dress. *Winterthur Portfolio*, 55(2–3), 121–185.

Wolf, E.R. (1982). *Europe and the people without history.* University of California Press.

5 Games

If the lives of people with whom we study are bound up with digital apps and games, then we also have a responsibility to engage them through these media. In the same way that anthropologists have turned to blogs to reach a public unlikely to pick up the monographs and the paywalled journal articles that make up the usual forms of anthropological dissemination, so too do anthropologists need to consider other platforms for their anthropological work (Stoller 2018). Games are one form that is instantly familiar and inherently participatory. In collaborative design, anthropologists and community participants make a world together through structured play. As a form of dissemination, games engage audiences in ways that other media cannot. Accordingly, this chapter will engage these possibilities for anthropological methods and for dissemination and public anthropology more than games as objects of anthropological inquiry.

There has been a long history of games in anthropology. Part of this is the universality of games and play to human and non-human life. The Pitt Rivers Museum has many examples of game pieces, game boards, balls, etc., collected (or taken) during the initial build-up of the collection in the 19th century, as does the Peabody Museum at Harvard and other museums around the world. And that catalog of 19th cultural alterity, The Golden Bough, references multiple games in its winding discussions of magic and religion – funerary games, Olympian games, festival games:

> In a Bohemian village near Koniggratz on Whit-Monday the children play the king's game, at which a king and queen march under a canopy, the queen wearing a garland, and the youngest girl carrying two wreaths on a plat behind him.
>
> (Frazer 1890/1935: 96)

For Frazer, games were "serious" – they were proof alongside magic, ritual, and sacrifice of the genealogies of European "civilization" he purported to trace through his kaleidoscope of folklore and (frequently) inaccurate ethnology. It is not therefore especially surprising that 20th century anthropologists would continue the study of games, and games studies continued apace

DOI: 10.4324/9781003330851-6

through the work of many of the Boasian anthropologists, with, for example, Mead studying games and children's play in her "Coming of Age in Samoa." And Mead and Bateson, as part of their efforts to aid the war effort, devised a game to help cultivate democratic values, "Democracy and Dictators," which was, however, never released.

In some ways, game studies in anthropology in the early 20th century still bore the imprint of an earlier, unilinear evolutionary past. For example, as Mathilda Coxe Stevenson writes of Zuni peoples:

> By enlightened people games are associated with sport and recreation. Among some primitive peoples games are played primarily for divination, but the ceremonial games of the Zuni are for rain, and they constitute an important element in their religion and society.
> (Stevenson 1903: 468)

That is, games may be universal, but "primitive" people lack the institutions of modern life that would consign games to worlds of leisure. That combination of cultural universals and racist, ethnocentric typologies characterizes much of the early discussion of games and culture

To an extent, this continues into anthropology's more "scientific" phases after World War II, in, for example, the usage of "experimental games" to test economic and cognitive thinking among people in small societies. Wiessner's 2009 study utilizes sessions of the "Dictator" and "Ultimatum" games among Ju/'hoansi peoples in order to understand practices of reciprocity and sharing against classical economic models premised on self-interest and competition (Wiessner 2009). While these "tests" yield interesting results regarding social mores in Ju/'hoansi society, they also contribute to an "othering" process where people are represented as somehow anterior to contemporary society, with self-interest confounding the altruistic proclivities of foraging peoples. Chibnik (2005) has noted some shortcomings in utilizing economic games to generate data about culture.

Other examples of games in anthropology have been more critical. For example, Angelini (2015) examines an elaborate role playing game (RPG) played in a Rio favela where people enact everyday life in their neighborhood – leading to powerful critiques of class and race-based inequalities in Brazil. There have been a number of ethnographic investigations of table-top role-playing games (TTRPGs) that have examined gender, race, capitalism, and competition in the context of play, along with ways that games suggest alternatives to neoliberalism (Mizer 2018).

But the biggest catalyst to games studies in anthropology has been more recent – the ubiquity of digital games and their growing importance in the lives of people. Although continuing "digital divides" means that digital games are experienced unequally, people in many of the places where anthropologists have done research are spending significant time with video and digital games – 8.5 hours per week in India, for example (The Economic Times 2021). Since these games construct a "gameworld" that is a more-or-less bounded space, anthropologists were quick to conceptualize them as "islands" in the style of older, 20th-century anthropology, as Boellstorff (2008) does in his appropriately titled "Coming of age in Second Life." Of course, games are hardly separate from everyday life and from global contexts, and many games studies also reflect the ways that digital games interact with work and social life in advanced capitalism (Rea 2018).

What all of these approaches agree on, though, is the relationship of games to life. Life is represented, modeled, and critiqued in games. Corporate games offer a version of life amenable to corporations; many indie games contest those hegemonies with alternatives to individualistic competition (Patkin 2021). And as we have argued about games in general, life (and anthropology) "is already a type of game, a goal-based modulation of experience through the use of rules" (Collins et al. 2022). In this context, "games" as we know them are simply more bounded cases of the games that make up human life.

Games and Multimodality

In many ways, games are the ultimate expression of a multimodal anthropology as we've defined it here. Bringing together multiple media (illustration, text, sound) in an interactive platform, games are immersive, not only bringing players into a "gameworld" but doing so in a profoundly tactile way, through dice, tokens, and game controllers. In that sense, games are the ultimate instantiation of sensory ethnography (Pink 2015). Table-top games are "cool media" that demand high degrees of participation, and that, through their design and mechanics, can offer exceptionally nuanced experiences of complex topics, through the vicissitudes of colonialism, through diverse identities, and oftentimes leading to profound realizations (Ouellette and Conway 2020). They are also one of the least explored avenues in multimodal anthropology. Although there are some "anthropology" and "ethnography" games available through "itch.io," these tend to be educational games (teaching concepts in anthropology) or anthropologically informed games (playing an alien studying the humans). A TTRPG game company – Anthropos games – for example, utilizes anthropological understandings of non-Western cultures and ecology to craft TTRPGs that diverge from the Eurocentric world of Dungeons & Dragons. Yet, even as games studies continue to proliferate in anthropology, games as a means of ethnographic dissemination remains relatively rare (but see Marin 2021).

Multimodal anthropological experiments with games fall into several broad categories: "games for teaching," "games for fieldwork," and "games for ethnography." Each of these is worth some discussion in the context of multimodality.

Games for Teaching

Pedagogical games in anthropology typically use game mechanics to instruct students in theory, methodology and "the canon." For example, Kuechling (2014) has developed a role-playing game called "The Tribe" which introduces students to institutions in New Guinea life, while Crawford et al. (2017) have developed "Loy Loy" to instruct students on microfinance in Cambodia. Many pedagogical games have a significant participatory component, and, as multimodal platforms, utilize a collaborative ethos to challenge hierarchies and canons in anthropology. Durington's "Cards Against Anthropology" builds on the popular card game "Cards Against Humanity" with frequently humorous options for ethical dilemmas, with the game designed to facilitate serious discussion of anthropology as an ethically fraught inquiry. Many of the ethical dilemmas and responses were contributed by students: the pedagogy, in other words, extends to game design as well as iterations of the game. The game is under a Creative Commons license just like "Cards Against Humanity" and has been translated into several other languages since its debut. Each iteration of gameplay welcomes even more ethical dilemmas that are central to the place and work of those who are using it in an iterative process building on the original design.

Games for Fieldwork

A number of games generate anthropological insights through play, including the various cognitive, psychological, and economic games discussed above. Games can open up discussion and foster an exchange of ideas that might be more difficult using interviews and semi-structured questions. In Candy and Watson's "The Thing From the Future," "The object of the game is to use the cards to generate the most interesting, funny or thought-provoking ideas for artifacts from the future" (Candy and Watson 2015). What "artifacts" are generated depend on other variables represented by other cards, including an overall theme (ARC cards) and context (TERRAIN cards). Of course, the biggest determinants of a "future" artifact are the people who play, and as a tool for ethnographic inquiry "The Thing From the Future" reveals a lot about the hopes and fears for the future, that, as a group exercise, would help people to unpack their assumptions and, perhaps, plan for alternatives. Similarly, we devised a game based on early text-based computer games where descriptions of rooms are followed by a limited number of choices for a player (e.g., "look in box"). Going around a small group of people who live or work together, each person describes a "room" illustrating some stereotypical institution or space, together with a couple of limited choices; the next person describes the next room, and so on. The game can generate insights into not only what people think their lives are like, but, frequently, critiques of the status quo (Collins et al. 2022).

Games as Ethnography

As a multimodal platform, games offer several advantages over conventional monographs. They are immersive, structuring both time and space during play (Wolf 2001). They are collaborative, and even single-player games require collaboration with the game designer – an agreement to play means a willingness to follow another's game mechanics. Finally, games are inherently ethical, in that they confront players with choices about how they should exist in that gameworld (Schrier and Gibson 2010). Accordingly, games can be a powerful platform for ethnographic dissemination.

Andrea Pia's "The Long Day of Young Peng" is a Twine game / interactive fiction that chronicles a single day in the life of a rural migrant (Young Peng) who moves from his village to work in Beijing. Peng is fictional – and his day is fictionalized – but he is based on people Pia interacted with during fieldwork on labor migration in China (Pia 2019). Through a variety of media, text narrative, ethnographic fieldnotes, photographs, films, and recordings, "The Long Day of Young Peng" presents a complex representation of one moment in the history of Chinese labor migration. The game excels at illustrating factors that might encourage people to leave their small villages, as well as the exploitation and discrimination faced by migrants as they begin a life "floating" between precarious day labor. More established Beijing residents tend to treat Peng badly – a measure of both the precarity of the migrants and the seemingly endless supply of cheap labor flocking to Chinese cities during this period.

"The Long Day of Young Peng" lacks the interactivity that comes with more immersive worlds, but the ethnographically intended media is rich in cultural insight into everyday life – e.g., the things in people's homes, or the different terms people use to describe labor migrants. Playing the game leaves one with a different understanding of social relationships and the logic of the choices people make in those contexts. And while representing these in a more traditional ethnography is certainly possible, writing by itself cannot approach the layers of meaning that a game affords. Of course, on a cursory level, people can click through the game and gain some insight into a labor migrant, but, at deeper levels, interactive multimedia lend themselves more to "thick description" than just textuality (Ryan 2015). This is even more the case when "thick description" is itself premised on the input from participants.

Designing a Game

Many of the games that people play – most of the market share of games, really – are designed by corporations, and represent the world in that context. This seems fairly obvious when we consider games like "The Game of Life," "Payday," and "Mystery Date," where "winning" hues closely to white, cisgender version of careers, family, and relationships (Patkin 2021). Even games like "Candyland" are complicit in teaching about consumption and desire; the goal of "play" is to, at least partly, reproduce social class and the hegemony of capitalism.

On the other hand, many of the tools to design games are more accessible than ever, courtesy of a wide variety of online resources. Materials for the production of homemade table-top games, of course, have always been accessible: cardboard, scissors, colored pencils. A number of small, print-on-demand companies that advertise on the internet have helped to facilitate more professional productions. With these, and more professional graphics accessible through open source applications like Inkscape, DIY game makers can produce professional-looking products that can rival the quality of commercial games.

Making video games is a more complex proposal with a steeper learning curve, although the scaled costs of Unity licenses allow non-professional designers some access to some of the same tools professionals use. Moreover, there are other, open-access platforms for game development, including Twine (see below) and some open-source engines (e.g., Godot). The other side to game creation is game distribution, and this, once again, is an area that has been inestimably aided by internet platforms. Itch.io is an indie game website where creators can make accounts and upload games (tabletop and digital) for sale, for free, or (most frequently) as a "pay what you want." The same business model exists in other analog to digital forms and markets such as vinyl records on Discogs. While anthropologists have been slow to post their games on these sites, there are nevertheless a number of anthropologically intended games available through sites like itch.io.

Hacking Games

You may not need to make a new game. After all, games can be hacked. Many instructors know the joy of throwing out 20 or so board games with missing parts and more than likely in the wrong boxes (if they exist) to a class of serious students and telling them to create a game in an hour based on their favorite anthropologist and their work. And there have always been "home rules" that represent alternatives to more corporate gameplay, from allowing younger children more chances, to entirely different games "ported" off of the same mechanics. This process has been facilitated by the development of Creative Commons licenses that allow for "adaptations" of content. "Cards Against Humanity" is a game created for profit, and one that involves the perpetuation of a number of racial and gender stereotypes under the general category of "non-PC" humor. That said, the game is also issued under a Creative Commons license (CC-BY-NC-SA 2.0) that allows for the game to be adapted for non-commercial purposes. Accordingly, there have been many other versions of the game created, using the same mechanics and card design, but altering the content, including "Cards Against Anthropology" (described in this chapter), "Cards Against Education Ethics," and "Cards Against Engineering Ethics" (Burkey and Young 2017).

Finally, many games allow for "modding," particularly open sandbox games like "Minecraft" where over 100,000 "mods" have been created – small changes that add objects, change the "look and feel," or allow for other functionalities, like the "imaginary" mod that allowed us to load fieldwork photos into a Minecraft "gallery" that we explore in a video ("Minecraft Multimodal") (Collins et al. 2022). Gigantic images of multimodal fieldwork float in the Minecraft air, and "we" (the anthropologists operating "Steve" through the Minecraft world), slowly maneuver around the gigantic installations, narrating our work as associate editors in the multimodal section of *American Anthropologist*. Other games can be modded in ways that add LGBTQIA+ content, or that utilize different cultural content in strategy or simulation games (Loban and Apperley 2019). Commercial game developers have reacted in a number of ways to modding – some encouraging the practice while others banning it (Postigo 2010). Again, similar to the vinyl record market, tensions exist over capital accumulation of creative activities in the move of a format from analog to digital production. Does one dissuade or encourage remixing (www.utpteachingculture.com/playing-theory-part-two/)?

Game Mechanics

According to Madsen (2017), game mechanics:

> determine both the means by which the player can act within the game world (for instance, pressing a designated button on a video-game controller to move from one kind of reality to another, or throwing dice in an analogue game) and also the constraints imposed on potential actions by the player (the legitimate movement of various chess pieces around the board, for example).
>
> (Madsen 2017: 80)

In other words, game mechanics are inherently ideological – they work to enable certain actions and behaviors while actively suppressing others. This gives game mechanics a particular importance in multimodal anthropology; they can reproduce or challenge the warp and weft of everyday life.

A few months ago, we read an article about an anthropologist who had designed a game collaboratively with an indigenous community. The game, the article explained, led players through a visionquest and featured indigenous language, storytelling, and music. As the article stated, the game was designed both by the community and for the community. Excited by this short essay, we eagerly searched for the published game and watched some game trailers. And here was the shock. Yes, the game included language and music and, yes, it seemed to trace the contour of this spiritual journey. But it was basically Super Mario – a horizontal side-scrolling game where players avoid monsters and vanquish various creatures for points. Of course, there's nothing wrong with these game mechanics *per se*, yet, we would argue, they still originate in particular ideological formations of linear narrative, individualistic agency, and, in particular, the antagonistic pitting of people against nature, displayed here as something to be either avoided or conquered. In short, the game mechanics themselves are part of a colonizing practice – the haptics of colonization (Cheng 2019). Even game controllers betray Western reification of agency and interaction in the limited choices allocated to the player – move forward, back, jump, shoot, grab; shorthand for the expansion of empire and the exploitation of the Global South (Galloway 2006).

On the other hand, many game designers and scholars have critically approached game mechanics. For example, Elizabeth LaPensée's "Thunderbird Strike" incorporates Anishinaabeg cosmology into the gameplay, including the directionality of the side-scrolling:

> The game scrolls in the opposite direction of conventional side-scrollers – moving from right to left, instead of left to right, in recognition of Anishinaabeg worldview, which looks at the Great Lakes to the South, and therefore envisions the journey from the Tar Sands to Line 5 as West to East.
>
> (LaPensée 2018: 32)

In addition, many games question the extractivist logic of conventional games: the money, points, territory that determine winners and losers. "Loy Loy" replaces the emphasis on personal acquisition with a game of cooperative savings set in a garment factory in Cambodia. The goal of the game is a collective one: save enough money so the group can purchase their own factory (loyloy.org): "If any player reaches bankruptcy, the game is over for everyone. All players are challenged to come together and reach the goal collaboratively to win, which you can do through extending loans to one another or paying one another's bills" (Mizer 2018).

So, while the game mechanics many of us grew up with attain a certain hegemony through their generic use, designing games through multimodal anthropology means thinking anthropologically about the entire process of game design. The temptation may be to simply replicate the mechanics of games with which you're familiar, but to do that is to risk reproducing powerful inequalities that, for example, elevate Lockean individualism over more collective forms – in the process undermining the power of games as a multimodal form. Since game design in multimodal inquiry needs this level of critical reflection, the process itself can be a powerful force of autoethnographic knowledge. It can also be part of a participatory design, bringing together anthropologists and people in the community in both game making and gameplay (see below).

An Example: Designing a Journaling Game

Journaling games are a variant of "choose your own adventure" role-playing, and represent a departure from many of the game mechanics common to the corporate gaming world. Since one is playing by oneself, "winning" is not defined in the same way – gameplay, and the creativity that might come from that, is the main reward in journaling games, even if there are point systems or levels or other elements of more individualistic gameplay.

Tim Hutchings's "Thousand Year Old Vampire" is a popular example of this subgenre, where players chronicle the "life" of a vampire through journal entries driven by prompts (Hutchings 2020). Players learn about the vampire's life as they play, with the result being a highly immersive and even moving experience. Like other RPGs, solo journaling resembles ethnographic methods in its emphasis on discovery and introspection (Petridis 2021). Here, RPGs are not far off from the anthropological project as a whole and suggest a fictional homology to autoethnographic practice; it is no surprise that autoethnography has been an important methodology in the world of game studies (Manning and Adams 2015).

As pedagogical tools, solo journaling games can help students develop skills in "thick description," and they can help even the most seasoned ethnographers develop questions for the field. In addition, solo journaling games can also be an ethnographic method by themselves. Presented with gameplay regarding familiar places and situations, people might journal their thoughts, in the process producing important ethnographic data about place and world-making, similar to "daily round" studies pioneered by Eliot Liebow and others (Liebow 1965; Gale and Wyatt 2019).

The following game was designed with all of these usages in mind, and also utilizes the powerful, peripatetic "Google Street View" app to generate gameplay. Here, we "misuse" an app, a practice that we explore in more detail in the next chapter. "Google Street View" famously includes unexpected detail: people captured in mid-gesture, open doors, found objects and other quotidian moments in urban life that appear in Street View quixotically. Together, these details prompt para-ethnographic narration, one that links together the perambulations of strolling through city streets into a storied order – de Certeau's "long poem of walking" appropriated into the app (de Certeau and Rendall 1988).

In order to work through the game design, we have used a worksheet devised by Nicholas Mizer, and available with a Creative Commons license on our "anthropologycon.org" website. The worksheet asks the would-be designer to think through each step in a design process, with the result being the prototype of an actual game, including an example of gameplay.

Game Design Worksheet for "The Man of the City"

Target Audience:
Anthropologists might use this game with interlocutors in the city where they live in order to generate data on daily life and the "daily round." In addition, anthropologists and anthropology students could play this game in order to stimulate questions for fieldwork. Finally, tourists and travelers could play this game in order to prepare for a trip.

Game Theme/Topic:
Edgar Allan Poe's story fragment "The Man of the Crowd" finds the narrator following an enigmatic person around a strange city for hours. The narrator never discovers the man's purposes in these peregrinations, but nevertheless advances several hypotheses.

Like the narrator in Poe's story, players in this game trace the movements and interactions of a person through Google Street View. As the person traverses their day, they meet people, build and maintain relationships, and accomplish their (unknown) goals.

The game deals with the experience of people in the city, and the dense relationships that people form.

Problem Statement:
The game places players in the position of residents of a strange city. Walking the city (through Google Street View), players encounter people they know, have conversations, and are witness to the ebb and flow of city life.
(For more on problem statements in game design, see Hiwiller 2016)

Game Design Worksheet

(Available at @anthropologycon / www.anthropologycon.org.)

High Level Concept
Core Dynamic:
The player needs to be able to describe their surroundings, imagine the context for situations, and write down what could happen. They also need to be able to ask questions around the details they see – questions that may have no answer, but that gesture to the many things we don't know about the world around us.

Format: Solo journaling game.
# of Players: 1
Facilitator Needed/Helpful? No
Player relationship: N/A
Time Required: As much time as people have to write and think.
Key Rules

a   Players begin by choosing a city. They can choose one they already live in, one they would like to visit, or they can choose a randomly selected city from a website like www.randomlists.com/random-world-cities. (Note: not every city is covered in Google Street View.)
b   Players go to that city on Google Map, and select Street View. They can place their token anywhere on the map to begin.
c   Once in the city, players roll a 6-sided die:

   1   1 = forward 1 (defined as the farthest the Streetview arrow can be extended in that direction)
   2   2 = forward 2
   3   3 = left 1
   4   4 = left 2
   5   5 = right 1
   6   6 = right 2

(If that direction is not possible on your map, roll again! If you roll the same number twice, you are interrupted in the street (see below).)

d   When you arrive at your location, rotate around to observe your surroundings. Write down details that you see.
e   Roll another 6-sided die for your motivation in going to this place.

   1   1 = To check on a friend
   2   2 = To check on a family member
   3   3 = To borrow something
   4   4 = To lend something
   5   5 = To pass along information
   6   6 = To receive information

Once you learn your motivation, explore what this might mean in your journal. Ask yourself questions about the things you don't know, or that you would need to know to explore this motivation in this place.

f   If you're interrupted in the street, roll another 6-sided die:

   1   1 = See an old friend
   2   2 = See an old teacher
   3   3 = See your romantic partner
   4   4 = Witness an incident (e.g., someone falls down)
   5   5 = Witness a spectacle (e.g., a sidewalk busker)
   6   6 = See something strange or unexpected

As with motivations, write down what this interruption might be in this place, and ask questions about what you might need to know.

g Continue exploring and journaling until you run out of time! (For more on core dynamics, see Kapp 2017.)

Design Considerations

- <u>What do the players do?</u> Look around, roll dice, and journal.
- <u>What interesting decisions will players face?</u> They will have to decide how to make sense of things that happen. In addition, they will try to enumerate what they don't know about this place.
- <u>What is the role of chance in the game?</u> Directions and events are decided randomly.
- <u>What resources do the players manage?</u> N/A.
- <u>What information is public to all players, known to some, known to none?</u> They know the name of the city, and they may have more in-depth knowledge of the place.
- <u>What hinders players?</u> What are the trade-offs? Places and events may not match exactly, and players will have to stretch their imaginations to make sense of them.
- <u>How does the game end?</u> Are there winning conditions? When the player runs out of time to play.

Adapted from Hiwiller (2016). For more on the role of chance and uncertainty, see Mizer (2017).

Explain a turn/segment or two of the game

1 The player generates a random city from a website – Wenzhou, China.
2 The player drops themselves on the map, and orients themselves on the street.
3 The player writes details of the scene – a busy, modern road with walls separating industrial buildings from the highway.
4 The player rolls a die – 1. Extend the arrow as far as it will go, and advance to that place.
5 The player rotates around to look, and sees that they are in front of a small factory.
6 The player rolls the die again – 4, to lend something.
7 At this point, the player may have several questions: What does this factory make? What would they want to borrow? Who would be in a position to lend something? Perhaps the player and the factory owner are both members of an informal, rotating credit association? And it's the factory owner's turn to collect?
8 All of these questions, and possible answers, go into the journal.
9 The player rolls again.

Games as Data

Playing this game might be, as we suggest above, a way to prepare for anthropological fieldwork – a means for cultivating different ways to look at things. In particular, the game is designed to stimulate questions: about place, relationships, and the ways these come together in a daily round of movement and sociality. It is also a way of collecting data.

There is a long history of utilizing games for ethnographic data. Sorting "games" have been used for decades to solicit folk categorization of plants, animals, and medicine. Others fall into the category of psychological tests, as in the various drawing activities that Mead introduced to children in Manus and elsewhere (Shankman 2021: 46). Children's games have, of course, been utilized as ethnographic data since the inception of anthropology in the 19th century (Schwartzman 1976). Using games as ethnographic data draws on this history, albeit in a more critical way. Games in older anthropology are largely extractive. Like other psychological tests, games in this context treat interlocutors as subjects to be experimented upon, as in, for example, the application of games from economics and social psychology to non-Western communities in order to measure their capacity for altruistic behavior (Gintis et al. 2003).

In multimodal anthropology, however, games – and the goal of their play – should be at once more transparent and more collaborative. In "The Man of the City," students may be able to formulate ethnographic questions and, in general, hone their sense of place. However, they are also producing data describing their "cognitive mapping" of a place – data that might inform their own sense of place in a way similar to asset mapping. As players journal their wandering, they are simultaneously producing rich, autoethnographic data on their constructions of place, meaning, and sociality (Sapach 2020).

Game design can be a powerful, multimodal tool. As a collaborative form, however, games need to be played, and, really, the only way to improve one's prototype is to playtest it. Starting in 2017, we have (along with several colleagues) sponsored a games workshop and salon called AnthropologyCon that gives anthropologists an opportunity to design and play anthropological games.

Building AnthropologyCon

As we describe above, games can be uniquely participatory and collaborative. They also set up a conundrum. If games are to be a useful, multimodal tool for anthropologists, then they need to be played. Where to play them? There are many places to disseminate games anthropologists have designed, among them the amazing itch.io site, which allows game creators to upload their work for free. Of course, the most powerful "dissemination" of games is gameplay itself. But where to go?

Nick Mizer began running RPG games at the American Anthropological Association Annual Meeting in 2015. He'd set up in the midst of the convention tumult, and, in a jarring intersection of academics and GenCon, GM a session. More formally, we held our first "AnthropologyCon" session in 2017 (with Mizer and others) at the AAA meetings in Washington, DC. There, we initiated a practice that we would reproduce in subsequent iterations in 2018, 2019, and 2022 – a workshop on game design followed by a gaming session. Over that time, we have had sessions on a variety of game platforms – table-top, digital, and AR. Our anthropological colleagues in Europe have followed similar directions, notably the European Association of Social Anthropology's 2020 Meeting in Lisbon, which hosted (virtually) a session on "Games as Urban Research."

There are many variables that can contribute to the success of a games workshop, but the most paramount is probably the willingness of participants 1) to collaborate together, and 2) to try things without the expectation of producing a "perfect" game. In our workshops, we design games together, which means, of course, that one person's vision cannot prevail without the input of others on their team. And games, as in other cases of multimodal practice, can only be developed through an iterative process of playtesting and re-design. As we describe above, game design itself is an ethnographic method, one that can tell us about the assumptions we bring into the field with regards to the individual, the life course, meritocracy, and to the limits of competitive individualism. This reflection should apply to the design process as well.

Classroom Exercises

1 Hack a game. Corporate games can be endlessly tweaked for pedagogical purposes. The best known examples are games like Monopoly, which have been utilized in sociology classrooms for decades to teach about stratification and inequality. In "Stratified Monopoly," people start off with distinct advantages over each other, and these compound over the course of the game (Fisher 2008). Any game can be hacked, and with a few modifications, that "Chutes and Ladders" board game gathering dust on your shelf can become an acerbic lesson in capitalist precarity. More anthropological "hacks" include games like "First Nations of Catan," which is an effective, and even devastating, interrogation of the settler colonialism at the heart of the popular table-top game, "Settlers of Catan" (Loring-Albright 2015).
2 This would also be one way of introducing digital games into class. Sandbox games like "Minecraft" can be modded in countless ways, and students can use them as foundations for their anthropologically intended games. Davies (2021) and many others have used Minecraft in their classrooms as a forum for hybrid instruction.

3   Engaging students in hacking their favorite games is an exercise that accomplishes at least two things: a) it helps students critique the hegemonic representations of self and others that are at the heart of corporate games; and b) it facilitates learning by asking students to apply critical concepts to game hacks and rule modifications.
4   Design a game. As in the example above, have students utilize Nick Mizer's "Game Design Worksheet" in order to design their own game. A great classroom exercise is to have students build games based on dynamics in ethnographies they're reading. Note that we're advocating "based on dynamics" rather than "based on actual peoples." Games always involve processes of abstraction, and the relationship of game to "reality" is never a one-to-one mapping (Harper et al. 2023). The danger here lies in both stereotyping peoples while at the same time advancing an impoverished representation of culture shorn of context and complexity. Ameliorating this means acknowledging that the goal of the game is not to "gamify" culture, but to teach anthropological concepts and to challenge students to think outside of their cultural assumptions. A game based on the discussion of Mauss's kula, for example, might concentrate on the kinds of reciprocity in Mauss's essay without actually mentioning the word "kula." Other games might speak to developing anthropological perspectives on problems, as does "Games Against Anthropology" (discussed above).
5   Play the game. Whether students have hacked or designed a game, the next stage should always involve playtesting. This can sometimes be accomplished during the class period, but it is also possible to find time to plan your own "AnthropologyCon" to playtest games your students have made.

References

Angelini, A. (2015). Ludic maps and capitalist spectacle in Rio de Janeiro. *Geofoum*, 65, 421–430.

Boellstorff, T. (2008). *Coming of age in second life: An anthropologist explores the virtually human.* Princeton University Press.

Burkey, D.D., & Young, M.F. (2017). *Work-in-progress: A "Cards Against Humanity"-style card game for increasing engineering students' awareness of ethical issues in the profession.* 2017 ASEE Annual Conference & Exposition, American Society for Engineering Education. Paper ID: 18520. DOI: doi:10.18260/1-2-29190.

Candy, S., & Watson, J. (2015). The thing from the future. http://library.teachthefuture.org.

Cheng, A.Y. (2019). *Playing nature.* University of Minnesota Press.

Chibnik, M. (2005). Experimental economies in anthropology. *American Ethnologist*, 32(2), 198–209.

Collins, S.G., Slover Durington, M., Gonzalez-Tennant, E., Harper, K., Lorenc, M., Mizer, N., & Salter, A. (2022). Ten things about anthropology games. *Anthropology News*, October 24. www.anthropology-news.org/articles/ten-things-about-anthropology-games.

Crawford, A., Fan, J., & Tankha, M. (2017). Loy Loy. http://loyloy.org.
Davies, D. (2021). Teaching digital anthropology through Minecraft. *The Geek Anthropologist*. https://thegeekanthropologist.com/2021/02/11/teaching-digital-anthropology-through-minecraft/.
de Certeau, M. & Rendall, S. (1988). *The practice of everyday life*. University of California Press.
The Economic Times. (2021). Indians spend an average of 8.5 hours gaming every week. https://economictimes.indiatimes.com/tech/tech-bytes/indians-spend-an-average-of-8-5-hours-gaming-every-week-report/articleshow/81506853.cms?utm_source=contentofinterest&utm_medium=text&utm_campaign=cppst.
Fisher, E.M. (2008). USA Stratified Monopoly: A simulation game about social class stratification. *Teaching Sociology*, 36(3), 272–282.
Frazer, J.G. (1890/1935). *The golden bough: A study in magic and religion*. The Macmillan Company.
Gale, K., & Wyatt, J. (2019). Autoethnography and activism. *Qualitative Inquiry*, 25 (6), 566–568.
Galloway, A. (2006). *Gaming*. University of Minnesota Press.
Gintis, H., Bowles, S., Byrd, R., & Fehr, E. (2003). Exploring altruistic behavior in humans. *Evolution and Human Behavior*, 24, 153–172.
Harper, K.M., Collins, S.G., Durington, M., Dumit, J., González-Tennant, E., Lorenc, M., Mizer, N.J., & Salter, A. (2023). Games and public anthropology. In H. Callan (ed.), *The international encyclopedia of anthropology*. Wiley.
Hiwiller, Z. (2016). *Players make decisions*. New Riders Press.
Hutchings, T. (2020). *Thousand year old vampire*. Petit Guignol LLC.
Kapp, S.B. (2017). Core dynamics: A key element in instructional game design. www.td.org/insights/core-dynamics-a-key-element-in-instructional-game-design.
Kuechling, S. (2014). Transforming classrooms into tropical islands. *Teaching Anthropology*, 4: 37–50.
LaPensée, E. (2018). Thunderbird strike: Survivance in/of an indigenous video game. *Video Game Art Reader*, 2(1), 28–37.
Liebow, E. (1965). *Tally's corner*. Rowan & Littlefield.
Loban, R., & Apperley, T. (2019). Eurocentric values at play. In P. Penix-Tadsen (ed.), *Video games and the Global South*. Carnegie Mellon University Press, pp. 87–100.
Loring-Albright, G. (2015). First Nations of Catan. *Analog Game Studies*, 9(4). https://analoggamestudies.org/2015/11/the-first-nations-of-catan-practices-in-critical-modification/.
Madsen, D.L. (2017). The mechanics of survivance in indigenously-determined videogames: Invaders and Never Alone. *Transmotion*, , 3(2), 79–110.
Manning, J., & Adams, T.E. (2015). Popular culture studies and autoethnography: An essay on method. *The Popular Culture Studies Journal*, 3, 187–122.
Marin, N. (2021). Huni kuin: Yube Baitana – An anthropological game adventure. *Multimodality & Society*, 1(4): 474–481.
Mizer, N. (2017). Lessons from Reiswitz. In S.G. Collins, J. Dumit, M. Durington, E. Gonzalez-Tennant, K. Harper, M. Lorenc, N. Mizer, & A. Salter (eds), *Gaming anthropology*. #AnthropologyCon, pp. 7–9.
Mizer, N. (2018). "Capitalism is so much easier!" Learning savings through playing a board game. *The Geek Anthropologist*. https://thegeekanthropologist.com/2018/01/26/capitalism-is-so-much-easier-learning-savings-through-playing-a-board-game/.

Ouellette, M.C., & Conway, S. (2020). A feel for the game: AI, computer games and perceiving perception. *Eludamos: Journal for Computer Game Culture*, 10(1): 9–25.

Patkin, T.T. (2021). Who's in the game? Identity and intersectionality in classic board games. McFarland.

Petridis, P. (2021). Anthropological role-playing games as multimodal pedagogical tools: Rhetoric, simulation and critique. *Entanglements*, 4(1), 107–125.

Pia, A. (2019). On digital ethnographies: Anthropology, politics and pedagogy (Part I). https://allegralaboratory.net/on-digital-ethnographies-anthropology-politics-and-pedagogy-part-i/.

Pink, S. (2015). *Mediated sensory ethnography*. Sage Publications. https://doi.org/10.4135/9781473917057.

Postigo, H. (2010). Modding to the big leagues: Exploring the space between modders and the game industry. *First Monday*, 15(5). https://firstmonday.org/ojs/index.php/fm/article/download/2972/2530.

Rea, S.C. (2018). Calibrating play. *American Anthropologist*, 120(3): 500–511.

Ryan, K.M. (2015). Beyond thick dialogue: Oral history and the "thickening" of multimedia storytelling. *Visual Communication Quarterly*, 22(2), 85–93.

Sapach, S. (2020). Tagging my tears and fears: Text-mining the autoethnography. *Digital Studies/Le champ numérique*, 10(1), 1–28.

Schrier, K., & Gibson, D. (eds) (2010). *Ethics and game design*. IGI Global.

Schwartzman, H.B. (1976). The anthropological study of children's play. *Annual Review of Anthropology*, 5, 289–328. www.jstor.org/stable/2949315.

Shankman, P. (2021) *Margaret Mead*. Berghan Books.

Stevenson, M.C. (1903). Zuni games. *American Anthropologist*, 5(3), 468–497.

Stoller, P. (2018). *Adventures in blogging: Public anthropology and popular media*. College of the Sciences & Mathematics Faculty Books. https://digitalcommons.wcupa.edu/ctsmfaculty_books/12.

Wiessner, P. (2009). Experimental games and games of life among the Ju/'hoan bushmen. *Current Anthropology*, 50(1), 133–138.

Wolf, M.J.P. (2001). *The medium of the video game*. University of Texas Press.

6 Apps

The Ubiquity of Apps

You are probably running apps right now. Even if you're reading a print edition of this, there's a smartphone nearby, perhaps an open laptop, and both of these devices are constantly running applications with or without your active participation, even if that means just "pinging" a cellular tower. For work, for school, for entertainment – we're surrounded by millions of differently useful applications.

To say that we utilize a variety of apps in our anthropological research is not an especially bold admission. Just as telephones were indispensable features for fieldwork during much of the 20th century, anthropologists today utilize a variety of apps in their work (including the telephone, which is now just one app among many). Notes, photographs, film, interviews, mapping, messaging, social media – all of these app-enabled tasks can be managed with a smartphone, and while the media content produced on our phones may not be of publishable quality, it is difficult to find an anthropologist who does not routinely utilize their phone to manage and conduct their ethnographic work.

There are, of course, some apps that have been specifically designed to facilitate ethnographic research. These are (mostly) apps to facilitate UX (user experience) and consumer research, often through enabling autoethnographies of consumer behavior using journals, video, and photographs. These would include apps like Indeemo's "Mobile Ethnography" and Special Design Research Studio's "Ethnography Journal." Others are the app extension of desktop software. Atlas.ti, for example, a well-known (and expensive) QDA (qualitative data analysis) software, published an app that allows for data collection and qualitative coding. Beyond these, there are a number of apps that anthropologists utilize in their fieldwork, even if they have not been designed for these functions (see below). Finally, a few anthropologists have designed their own applications, customized to their fieldsites, their methods, and, ultimately, their theoretical orientations.

Yet apps are not just a *tool*. They can facilitate and enable research. They can also channel our ideas and, within the structures of apps, prevent certain kinds of thinking and ideas. In other words, apps display a certain

DOI: 10.4324/9781003330851-7

amount of agency, an idea familiar to students of Bruno Latour and Actor Network Theory. As Ilahiane (2022: 4–5) explains:

> In Latour's view, no difference should be made between humans and artifacts; all are actors, or "actants," that are able to act, mediate, delegate, compose, extend, and influence. Actants are given competencies, that is, powers and capacities to act. The competencies of actants in a setting cannot be determined in advance but can only be attributed to them as the result of their being embedded in a network of human and nonhuman entities.

If, as Haraway has suggested, late-modern machines are "disturbingly lively," then none are more lively (or more disturbing) than the dozens of applications that run simultaneously on our phones, recording, mapping, scanning, and (worryingly) sending information back to corporations for third-party resale (Haraway 1989). And if these "lively" machines are imbued with agency, then that agency needs to be acknowledged in the anthropological work that we do, as anthropologists have done with the camera and other technologies (Edwards 2015). More than just other "tools," the apps we use privilege certain ethnographic moments and particular regimes of representation. As a table upon which we (methodologically) perform anthropology, it's worth asking what else our apps are up to.

The Theory of Affordances

One helpful concept connects the insights of early Actor Network Theory to app design itself: affordances. Understood by some technologists as simply the functions that a technology can accomplish (Gibson 2014), the concept has grown to encompass a more relational model, "neither solely an independent property of the object itself, nor is it exclusively an intentional state within the mind of the person engaging with it, but a relational property between object and agent" (Knappett 2004: 46). That is, affordances are much more than a series of functions that can be designed into a device like apples in a basket; the concept describes a network linking user and function with tasks in the world (Bucher and Helmond 2017). Importantly, this is more than a dyad (user + function). Whenever we consider an application, we also must consider the relationship of affordances to each other. Which ones can be used together? Which affordances do IT devices seem to prefer? Twitter (now "X"), for example, combines text with options to include photos, videos, gifs, and geolocation. Within the textbox, one can include an "@" to "mention" someone, a "#" to add a hashtag, etc. These are all functions, certainly, but they are not connected together in the same way. For example, media cannot be linked together without text. In other words, if I tweet a photograph of a protest, and you tweet a photo of the same protest, there is no way to link them without text (not that uploading EXIF data would be a good thing!). All of the connections in Twitter are enabled through text. And not all media files are as easily supported. While there is (as we write this) a voice recorder on the iOS version of Twitter, there is still no way to (directly) upload the audio file.

When anthropologists utilize Twitter – or any app – they participate in this networked production and in the path dependencies introduced through these networked connections (and disconnections). This combining and moving between linked media is one of the foundational characteristics of multimodality, and it is one of the characteristics of multimodality that differentiates it from multimedia. These interconnections are most obvious in something like app affordances, where functions are yoked together in order to accomplish tasks. For anthropologists, the most important elements include: 1) the production of content; 2) its connection to other content; and 3) its connection to other users. Mapping, film, photography – all of these have a long history in anthropology, but apps organize, structure, and communicate that content in ways that impact the research we do. As Casey O'Donnell writes of dependence on "Evernote" in fieldwork, "In the case of a mobile app tool like Evernote, it is easy to see the dualism of mobile apps using us, while we use various mobile apps" (Collins et al. 2017: 113). Our apps "use" us in ways that profoundly shape the course of fieldwork. Facebook, for example, implies networks of connections, linked media and what Gergen describes as "absent presence" (Gergen 2002). And while Facebook may deepen the connections between a fieldworker and a community through a variety of shared media content, the platform makes it more challenging to "leave" the field – if only in a sense of temporary closure necessary to finish ethnographic writing and media (Gerson et al. 2017).

Apps are also windows onto the digital divide. Whether "free" or not, the most widespread apps are controlled by corporations that commodify and monetize users and user data in ways that may influence their behaviors and social relationships. For example, there have been many studies on the "echo chambers" that Facebook constructs through targeted news feeds and through self-affirming groups that circulate conspiracies among themselves in a positive feedback loop with devastating effects on power and politics (Del Vicario et al. 2016). When Facebook effectively monopolizes online activity, as it has done in under-served communities where they offer "free" internet access through their app, it's worth asking what impacts these filters have on the ways people see themselves and their communities (Nemer 2022). When anthropologists work with people in ethnographic research with Facebook as a platform for their communication, to what extent are they complicit in the platform's commodification and reifications?

In other words, apps are characteristic of the ethical dilemmas of multimodality. They are problematic not because they are ontologically more ethically questionable, but because their multiagency makes their ethics more visible. We cannot help but ask about ethics when the platform is shared by people with differential access and controlled by corporations who explicitly profit off of user data and sell their audience to anyone wanting to buy it.

(Not) Designing an App

We started incorporating app design into our work almost ten years ago. Since then, we have published exactly zero apps. While we have prototyped apps, contributed to several app designs, and have worked on a variety of wireframing tools and with MIT App Inventor, authoring apps has never been the end-goal of our multimodal anthropology (Durington et al. 2015). Why? There's time and cost, certainly (more on this below), but also the knowledge that there are a lot of great apps already in the world: reportedly almost 3 million for Android devices and 2 million for Apple. If we've looked hard enough, we've always been able to find apps that have met our needs, even if they need to be "misused" (see below). That said, we have found the app design process to be important to a truly collaborative, multimodal anthropology.

Many researchers doing community work (both inside and outside of anthropology) include app design in their research prospectus. Over more than a decade of peer review for interdisciplinary research grants, we have read many, many proposals for apps. Over the past ten years, apps have become one of the "deliverables" in interdisciplinary research. Like all apps, these are baskets into which affordances were to be placed, and the app itself would be a connective technology, allowing, for example, citizen scientists to document alien plant species, gym-goers to maximize workouts, social media connections between homebound people, etc. Yet as much as app development makes sense, one of the questions we have returned to again and again is: do you really need to make an app? A few years ago, a community group approached us for help designing an app. Full disclosure: we're not app designers, nor are we coders. But we work with people in these areas, and we asked them. How much would it cost? In their case, given the complexity of functions, data storage requirements – perhaps US $200,000. And that's not including continued maintenance and upgrades. In all, an expensive proposition. Of course, some anthropologists have done this, to great effect.

"EthnoAlly" is a fieldwork app designed by Paolo Favero. Produced for multimodal fieldwork, it brings together mapping, photos, video, and text in ways that track closely with the workflow of the anthropologist. EthnoAlly is the response of anthropologists to the fundamentally multimodal nature of fieldwork, building connections back into what threatens to spiral into disconnected multimedia. The inspiration for EthnoAlly came from walking with his father in their ancestral village in Italy:

> As his father started telling stories, Favero decided to activate the voice recorder on his iPhone (with his father's permission). He also took several snapshots of the places his father would point out to him. Indeed, he did not record any notes, but used his voice as a kind of track, repeating key names in order to remember them later on. At

some point during this promenade, Favero decided to activate a movement tracker (*Runtastic*, a runners' app) in order to keep a memory of their route, which was progressively getting more complicated. But all of these technologies together made him lose his father and the intensity of the conversation. What if a single tool could actually coordinate that work so that the recorder of stories could stay with the storyteller?

(Favero and Theunissen 2018)

The app here is a material instantiation of multimodal philosophy – a digital tool for the documentation of data from multiple senses. Enabling more peripatetic and spontaneous fieldwork encounters, EthnoAlly can help to build a "critical awareness of the sensory and affective character of our lifeworlds" (Favero and Theunissen 2018: 165).

But do you need to make an app? And what would that look like? When we've worked with communities on their technology needs, they are frequently interested in app development, but have only hazy ideas about what the app should look like. They know the desired end – i.e., what tasks the app should facilitate, and the ways it will help the community, but the affordances themselves, and the ways these are connected together, are not as clear. People know what they want – and anthropologists need to honor their expertise. But that does not mean that people are ready to decompose those wants into the algorithmic flow of app design.

"Wireframing" is a part of UX where the functionality of the app (or the webpage or the game) is mapped out not only as a series of tools, but in terms of the user's experience of them – the flow that will proceed from a screen or one affordance to the next. You can wireframe your app in order to start planning and visualizing. You can do this on a whiteboard, of course, but there are a number of wireframing tools available that will help anthropologists visualize their app and sketch out its functionality. Moreover, these tools are especially important in collaborative and participatory design (see below), and there is a robust literature on their application in all kinds of user-centered research (Hamm 2014).

One of the best tools we've used in app design is the venerable MIT App Inventor, a web-based application that allows users to create apps using blocks of code, something that MIT pioneered with the development of Scratch in the early 2000s. The usefulness of this application, however, extends to wireframing itself. To be clear, App Inventor is designed to do just that: take people through a process where they design and use apps. The vast gallery for App Inventor apps is testament to the success of the easy, intuitive approach to programming and to the success of this OA project. However, App Inventor's graphic interface also works well for wireframing.

Let's say that we're working with a community group regarding environmental justice. Since poor and working class neighborhoods are also often sites of environmental pollution, working class communities bear the added burden of undesirable health outcomes from environmental pollution on top of other race- and class-based inequalities (Fabricant 2023). But taking people's lived experiences and translating them for outsiders to understand is a challenge – something an app might help with. Convening a design group from the community, we start to list off the different things the app should do. It should, for example, allow users to photograph and geolocate visible environmental pollution, and to add notes contextualizing the photographs or other visual media using other senses (e.g., smell). Furthermore, the data should be collaborative – the map should show the sites that others have encountered.

From the results of this discussion, we can next break people up into small groups and have them model what the app should look like using MIT App Inventor. The interface utilizes a very simple "drag and drop" for different features; people can add the affordances that will allow them to accomplish their goals, as in Figure 6.1.

In this quick mock-up of the "Trash Mapper" app, we have some simple elements that have been arranged vertically on the screen. First, a map that allows geolocation. Beneath that, a text box for note taking. Finally, some functions that are not themselves part of the visual interface: a cloud database component that would allow data to be stored and shared, a "sharing" component for sending data to each other via email or social media, and a camera component that will allow people to take a picture.

This looks great, but we should remember that this isn't an app until we've actually programmed these functions. That's in the "blocks" screen, which involves piecing together programming "chunks" that will allow the affordances of the app to work together. Importantly, we have not programmed anything here, and it's a good bet that something this complex

Figure 6.1 Screenshot of Trash Mapper in MIT App Inventor

would be a big challenge using MIT App Inventor. Still, as a wireframing tool, this helps people to start visualizing what they need, and to begin the process of converting their heterogeneous goals into app affordances. And it is an iterative process. If we re-convene our small groups and go through what we've done, people may note that there are no interfaces on this illustration that would allow us to take a photograph or share our results. If we add those buttons, will it make the screen too busy? Do we need another screen?

Another useful technique is to map the flow of affordances, again as a participatory tool. While there are numerous wireframing tools that would allow us to do this, we have found networking applications like Gephi to be especially helpful (and free).

In the simple network diagram shown in Figure 6.2 we can see the flow of these functions. On opening the app (A), users would locate the source of environmental pollution on a map (B). From there, they would pin the map with the exact location (C), photograph the site (D), and write notes (E) contextualizing the photograph and elaborating on other senses (smell, hearing) not visible in the photograph. Finally, the user would share the site with others using email and/or social media (F) and, lastly, submit the site to the cloud database (G), where it might be viewed by other members of the team (H).

The flow here is simple and linear. Note that the user is not required to do all three of the affordances (mapping, photograph, and notes) before submitting the data. Note, also, that there is no function here that would allow for others to edit or comment on other user's submissions – which would, theoretically, be visible on the shared map. Would that be another screen? Another set of functions? By bringing people through the process of translating their desiderata into affordances, we not only begin to arrive at a realistic vision about what such an app should look like, but also how such an app might be built.

This would be, perhaps, the next step in the process: engaging someone to help you build the app. Prototyping the app on App Inventor is something that anyone can do – with a little work. This prototype, though, is likely to be a much scaled-down version of what people in the community had in mind. To do more than this, you would probably want to bring in people

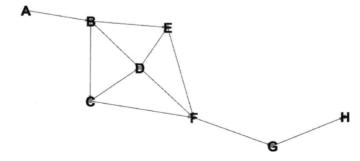

Figure 6.2 Gephi network map

with expertise in Java and Android environments. These people may well originate outside of the community. Although multimodal anthropology is inherently collaborative and participatory, the boundaries of that collaboration need to be constantly negotiated. In other words, who are the stakeholders? The anthropologist, certainly, alongside the community involved in a fight for environmental justice. And, of course, all of the people who might be the audience for these data. But what about the app developer? Or an app development company? Translating a vision that is the result of a participatory design process into a completed product involves a number of negotiations; not everyone will share the intentions of the anthropologist and community – and, of course, there may be considerable variation here as well.

While it seems likely that anthropologists will continue to develop apps for their work, we believe a more reasonable approach is to utilize extant apps that can be re-purposed for anthropology.

What's to stop you from utilizing one in your work?

App Misuse

If you've ever utilized "Map My Run" or something similar in order to record your transect walks through communities. If you've picked through Facebook groups in order to identify community leaders to contact. If you've conducted "interviews" over WhatsApp. We've got news for you. You have "misused" an app. Farman defines "creative misuse" as "imagined uses and daily practices of a technology" (Farman 2014: 331). In Farman's example a GPS surveillance app is transformed into a classroom game where students try to guess the word you're spelling out as you move around the campus in real time. We have misused many apps, from mapping and tourism apps to all kinds of social media. We submit that a misused app may be able to accomplish many of the things you want, without the heavy cost in money and time. The beginning stages of this process remain the same and, if anything, opting to misuse an existing app underscores the importance of delineating the needs of the community and deciding on particular affordances. Misusing an existing app can mean "taking back" its relevance to a community – typically one that has had no say in the initial design of the app at all.

Let's re-visit the participatory design sessions that resulted in the wireframe for "Trash Mapper." The goal was to geolocate pollution on a collaborative map, upload photographs or other media, and write notes that contextualized those findings. Note that we lead here with the community needs assessment. Are there other apps that might meet these needs? Northwestern University's Knight Lab offers a variety of free, digital storytelling tools, among them "StoryMap," a free and scaled-down version of geo-located storytelling applications. Knight Lab's StoryMap supports photographs, but you can include hyperlinks, and embed video and audio links. And, rather than true geolocation (utilizing GPS coordinates), StoryMap requires you to move around your pin on OpenStreetMap until you're happy

118 *Apps*

Figure 6.3 Trash Mapper StoryMap

with its location. Finally, these maps can be shared, simply through the artifice of having a single account that everyone can use to update the map.

In the version of "Trash Mapper" shown in Figure 6.3, a red pin on the map would correspond to some site where pollution has been logged by a member of the team.

As we've discussed previously, this creative misuse does not come without ethical dilemmas. With StoryMap, you're uploading your data to an external institution who maintains control over the platform. And while the researchers on this project can keep this as a draft, if published it would be visible by others who may not share the community's commitment to environmental justice. There is also the issue of the ephemerality of the platform. Knight Lab has maintained this free platform for over ten years. Will that always be the case? Later, we will discuss the ephemerality of multimodality, but the limited lives of apps underscores the necessity for back-ups.

Other Apps

In the example above, a decision to utilize StoryMapJS comes directly from needs assessment with a community: the app incorporates the affordances articulated by people in the community. On the other hand, sometimes apps suggest affordances which open up new possibilities for engagement and interaction. ZOME is a free, AR app designed by Theodore Wohng (https://zome.app). With this, users can place a variety of media at geolocated places to be found by people in the user's "friends" group, although there is also a "public" option for content that anyone can see. For example, in the "capsule" in Figure 6.4, we have a

Apps 119

Figure 6.4 ZOME screenshot

placed a photo at a church in Baltimore where we undertook community-based research last summer.

People utilizing the app can search the area and be alerted to the AR content. For an alternative to "Trash Mapper," this would enable users to pin commentaries and other media directly on the sources of environmental pollution in the area. And, like Knight Lab's StoryMap application (above), a team can share the same login information to work on something together. In this case, ZOME in some ways exceeds the design specifications from the community and suggests other affordances – more peripatetic, certainly, but also possibly more critical.

Twine

In this last section, we want to bring together games and applications. "Twine" is a storytelling platform that utilizes a non-linear "choose your own adventure" structure composed of "passages" connected to each other, like nodes in a network. Like a network, Twine brachiates immediately into two overlapping functions: it supports a way of writing, and it supports games.

Over the past year, we have been working with the National Park Service on an ethnographic project at Ellis Island, the major port of entry (and of deportation) for European immigrants and others into the United States from 1892 until its closure in 1954. In 1965, Ellis Island became part of the State of Liberty National Monument under the control of the National Park Service (Eleey et al. 2000). While interpretations of the site have mainly centered on European immigration, many other stories could be told, among them people employed on the island, and people who were denied entry there – especially after the 1924 National Origins Act (Pelayo 2014). Generally, interpretations of immigration at Ellis Island have amounted to affirmation of what Matthew Frye Jacobson calls "Ellis Island whiteness": "myths and symbols of distinctly *immigrant* whiteness jostled with the older icon of WASPdom" (Jacobson 2006: 7).

Part of our work there involves archival research in efforts to highlight more diverse and more inclusive experiences of immigration. But as multimodal anthropologists, we feel strongly that this process cannot be "top-down"; we have no interest in trying to "force" site interpreters to replace their more Eurocentric narratives with ours. As with other multimodal projects we've engaged, this, too, needs to be collaborative.

We began the process with meeting with park rangers and other stakeholders, each of whom discussed their approaches to interpreting the site, the ways these have changed over the years, and the directions they would like to see them going in the future. Rangers recognized several overlapping problems, among them the relative paucity of non-white experiences in their tours, a deficit which has been thrown into bold relief in the face of a growing diversity among park visitors. Furthermore, they recognized that post-1965 immigration looks very different than the early-20th-century heyday of Ellis Island. How, in other words, can Ellis Island, home to the National Immigration Museum, speak to the changing face of immigration to the United States? And how can the site better acknowledge the experiences and the challenges of non-European immigration in the early 20th century?

Fortunately, the archival record yields other possibilities in the Ellis Island archives that might suggest other narratives, including materials relating to Jamaican-born immigrants employed as seamstresses on the island (see Figure 6.5).

Could these help build alternative narratives? Perhaps – but, again, only in a collaborative forum. As we explain in our design chapter, participatory design is indissociable as a multimodal method.

Twine 2 was released in 2014, as both a download and as an online interface that could be programmed in your browser. The ease of this interface made it especially attractive for participatory design. Users need neither software nor

Apps 121

Figure 6.5 Archival material from Ellis Island of a Jamaican-born immigrant employed as a seamstress on the island

coding experience and, indeed, users of the web-based platform need only know a couple of basic commands to get started on their Twine game.

In this example, the only knowledge users need is the double bracket command "[[... .]]" which initiates a new passage. With this version of Twine, there is very little standing in the way of participation. If you have a Wi-Fi connection, and can type, then you can design a Twine.

In order to make this a participatory exercise, we convened workshops with stakeholders and presented them with folders of archival materials documenting the stories of people whose experiences intersected with Ellis Island – immigrants, deportees, detainees, employees. We charged them with ordering these materials into a narrative that they would be comfortable delivering to a group of park visitors. We then demonstrated some of the basic functionalities of Twine, and had them structure their "tours" using the choose-your-own-adventure style to simulate the difficult and oftentimes impossible choices open to people. Of course, there is only one "true" choice: the fate of actual people. We are working from archival documents, after all. Alternatives could be prefaced with "Although they didn't choose to do this, if they had their situation would have been…"

For our project, the result is an intuitive, easy-to-follow "tour" that focuses on some of that complexity, one that avoids over-generalization by focusing on the specific, documented stories of people who immigrated – or tried to immigrate.

122 *Apps*

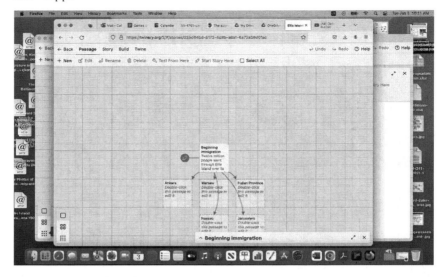

Figure 6.6 Screenshot of Twine

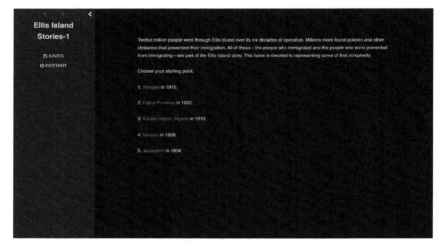

Figure 6.7 Screenshot of Twine game

Classroom Exercises

1   Misuse an app. This activity works well as a brainstorming activity.

    a   Have students find apps they have in common on their phones.
    b   Arrange them in groups based on these commonalities.

    c   Give each group the task of designing ethnographic research around this application.
    d   Have each group report on their proposed project.

Students are generally able to find interesting research projects around many apps that would not be normally used in ethnographic work: shopping apps, food delivery, streaming music.

2. Twining your life.

    a   Have students go to twinery.org and open up a browser-based version of Twine.
    b   As a class, brainstorm on common experiences people have had (e.g., first date, first day on the job), and divide students into groups based on their common experiences.
    c   Make a "game" of the experience using Twine's passages to delineate stereotypical situations and choices.

References

Bucher, T., & Helmond, A. (2017). The affordances of social media platforms. In J. Burgess, T, Poell, & A. Marwick (eds), *The Sage handbook of social media*. Sage Publications, pp. 233–253.

Collins, S., Durington, M., Favero, P., Harper, K., Kenner, A., & O'Donnell, C. (2017). Ethnographic apps/apps as ethnography. *Anthropology Now*, 9(1), 102–118.

Del Vicario, M., Vivaldo, G., Bessi, A.*et al*. (2016). Echo chambers: Emotional contagion and group polarization on Facebook. *Scientific Reports*, 6, 37825. https://doi.org/10.1038/srep37825.

Durington, M., Collins, S.G. & 2014 Anthropology by the Wire Collective. (2015). Games without frontiers. In A. Gubrium, K. Harper, & M. Ontanez (eds), *Participatory visual and digital research in action*. Left Coast Press, pp. 259–276.

Edwards, E. (2015). Anthropology and photography: A long history of knowledge and affect. *Photographies*, 8, 1–18. DOI: doi:10.1080/17540763.2015.1103088.

Eleey, P., Gonshorowski, M., & Uschold, D. (2000). *Cultural inventory landscapes: Ellis Island Statue of Liberty National Monument*. National Park Service.

Fabricant, N. (2023). *Fighting to breathe*. University of California Press.

Farman, J. (2014). Creative misuse as resistance. *Surveillance & Society*, 12(3), 377–388.

Favero, P.S.H., & Theunissen, E. (2018). With the smartphone as field assistant: Designing, making, and testing EthnoAlly, a multimodal tool for conducting serendipitous ethnography in a multisensory world. *American Anthropologist*, 120(1), 163–167.

Gergen, K.J. (2002). The challenge of absent presence. In J.E. Katz & M. Aakhus (eds), *Perpetual contact: Mobile communication, private talk, public performance*. Cambridge University Press, pp. 227–234.

Gerson, J., Plagnol, A., & Corr, P. (2017). Passive and active Facebook use measure (PAUM): Validation and relationship to the reinforcement sensitivity theory. *Personality and Individual Differences*, 117, 81–90. DOI: doi:10.1016/j.paid.2017.05.034.

Gibson, R. (2014). Narrative hunger. *Cultural Studies Review*, 20, 4052.

Hamm, M.J. (2014). *Wireframing essentials*. Packt Publishing.
Haraway, D. (1989). A manifesto for cyborgs. In E. Weed (ed.), *Coming to terms*. Routledge.
Ilahiane, H. (2022). *The mobile phone revolution in Morocco: Cultural and economic transformations*. Lexington Books.
Jacobson, M.F. (2006). *Roots too*. Harvard University Press.
Knappett, C. (2004). The affordances of things: A post-Gibsonian perspective on the relationality of mind and matter. In E. DeMarrais, C. Gosden, & C. Renfrew (eds), *Rethinking materiality: The engagement of mind with the material world*. McDonald Institute for Archaeological Research, pp. 43–51.
Nemer, D. (2022). *Technology of the oppressed*. MIT Press.
Pelayo, M. (2014) *Producing heritage, remaking immigration*. PhD thesis, University of South California.

7 Design

Design means re-imagining anthropology as well. If we would like to "restore design to the heart of anthropology's disciplinary practice" (Ingold and Gatt 2013: 140), then we must also dismantle the hoary dichotomies that have undermined possibilities for an anthropology defined by political practice. Doing this may be achievable through a design anthropology infused with a Bloch-ian hope for alternative possibilities. And through this, we may be able to sketch the possibility for an anthropology that engages what it really means to be human, i.e., to be a person desirous of a better world. This chapter considers design as a future horizon for a multimodal anthropology, one premised on deep collaboration and a transformative ethos.

We agonized over where to place this penultimate chapter. Is design anthropology an example of multimodal anthropology? Is it a basket in which we might locate diverse multimodalities? Is it the basis of multimodal anthropology itself? We tend toward the last of these. To the extent that multimodal anthropology is truly collaborative, then it must be premised on a design anthropology, which, by definition, involves outcomes that are the product of horizontal, collaborative processes and that are oriented toward achieving the goals of the community. It appears here, toward the end of the book, in order to underscore the ways in which all of the preceding chapters have also been premised on design. Photographs, games, apps – all of these remain exercises in multimedia unless they are embedded in collaborative processes that make them both the product of the group and a materialization of ethnographic work.

Participatory Action Research

One of the enduring legacies of Sol Tax is the proliferation of various forms of participatory action research (PAR) in anthropology (including "community based research" and "action research"), a collaborative and iterative approach that is used in multiple disciplines, in academic settings, NPOs, NGOs and in government (Sousa 2022). It is not, as many PAR advocates point out, a method (Kindon et al. 2009), although it has been written about as if it was a distinct methodology:

DOI: 10.4324/9781003330851-8

Second, PAR has proven to be a powerful approach for working with subordinate or oppressed groups to better their circumstances within society. In this respect it has become a methodology of the marginal that has promoted the interests of the poor and disenfranchised. This has primarily been effected through the inclusion of these groups within the key decision-making procedures of the research process and their ownership of its outcomes.

(Jordan 2003: 186)

An "approach," though, is not a method *per se*; certainly, PAR isn't premised upon particular kinds of data, nor is it associated with analytical or interpretative techniques. It is, perhaps, better to think of PAR as an approach that interrogates methodologies, which it incorporates in an eclectic way that is, perhaps, quite familiar to anthropology. "Interrogates" here refers to the way PAR seeks to redress power inequalities in order to collaborate with communities to effect positive change. If we consider anthropological methods as inherently unequal and the ethnographic enterprise as a research method arising in the space of colonial encounter, then "decolonization" must include challenges to methods alongside the necessity of challenging the anthropological canon and faculty hiring practices (Gupta and Stoolman 2022). And since it exists in the space of critique and dialectical transformation, it seems self-defeating to fix a definitive definition of PAR. It is a method, perhaps, of overcoming and transformation. It defines research as a problem, one whose solution involves deep collaboration, "thick solidarity" and an iterative process that represents considerable time and commitment: "that is, a kind of solidarity that mobilizes empathy in ways that do not gloss over difference, but rather pushes into the specificity, irreducibility, and incommensurability of racialized experiences" (Liu and Shange 2018: 190). PAR problematizes the research process, forces it into reflection and negotiation, not only to the point where there are demonstrable results, but into the afterlife of research as communities work toward positive change in research collaborations.

It is also resolutely multimodal, and includes not only methods that we might associate with conventional ethnography (participant observation, interviews), but also methods that have more salience to people in the communities where anthropologists might work – mapping resources, using photovoice to articulate problems and solutions, building exhibits to communicate concerns with government groups and non-profits. Actually, PAR (in its various incarnations) is what extends multimodal anthropology beyond multimedia – it is multimedia that arise through negotiated and collaborative research, and that are directed toward critical reflection and positive change. PAR is what helps to mitigate against a revanchist multimodal anthropology that replaces "visual anthropologist-as-auteur" with "content creator-as-auteur," and that preserves all of the hierarchical relations that have privileged certain voices over others.

That critical reflection begins with the recognition that anthropology develops in the context of colonialism and racial inequality, and that the anthropological encounter has been a subset in a larger narrative of Western domination and the subjugation of peoples deemed "other" by the West (Wolf 1982; Fabian 2002). Challenging that past should mean many things, but in PAR it means surrendering the authority that anthropologists have claimed over the representation of others, the hubris that we could understand people's lives more than they themselves. This is a big challenge, especially when that hubris has been elevated to methodology, and its practitioners enshrined in the anthropological canon. As Geertz writes of the superiority of anthropological theory over that of the anthropologist's subjects:

> In one sense, of course, no one knows this better than they do themselves; hence the passion to swim in the stream of their experience, and the illusion afterward that one somehow has. But in another sense, that simple truism is simply not true. People use experience-near concepts spontaneously, unself-consciously, as it were colloquially; they do not, except fleetingly and on occasion, recognize that there are any "concepts" involved at all.
>
> (Geertz 1974: 587)

That is, in terms both oblique and theoretical, the colonizing mind at the heart of ethnography: the certainty that anthropological truths are inaccessible to people who live them. This is the sharpest break between PAR methodologies and more conventional ethnographic methods. As Lamphere (2018: 72) summarizes:

> The major tenant is that community members are equal partners in all phases of the research, from problem definition to data collection, interpretation, and dissemination. Knowledge is not owned by the researchers but shared and retained by the community. The research process should empower community members through capacity building and power sharing in terms of both decision making and knowledge production.

There are several parts to this: 1) anthropologists work to combat hierarchies that may arise during the research process; 2) while producing knowledge that is owned by the community; and that 3) contributes to the community's overall goals.

In practice, this means that sometimes there is no research. We've built up relationships with community leaders, attended workshops, meetings, church services, Zoomed with everybody, but still, no project arises – perhaps because one of the three conditions has not been met. Perhaps people are unsure of our motives, or worried that the knowledge we produce will ultimately be appropriated into uses that are inimical to the community's goals. Most likely, though, the problem is that we may all be on the same page, but a project utilizing our skill sets and that meets community needs has not arisen. In this case, the best way to help is to find PAR colleagues who might better meet their needs.

Multimodal Anthropology and Design

Ostensibly, design would seem like an unlikely extension of PAR. After all, we live in a world of top-down design, and we face the daily repercussions of a world that was not only not designed by the people consigned to live in that world, but was actually designed *against* people. "Hostile design," for example, describes urban spaces that have been specifically engineered against their use by people defined as "undesirable": park benches with armrests down the middle and spikes on display window ledges (Rosenberger 2017). These, however, are only the most visible products of hostile design. There are also laws against loitering, sleeping outdoors, panhandling, busking. Highways like Baltimore's "highway to nowhere" slice through neighborhoods, leaving broken lives and destroyed communities in their wake (Phillips de Lucas 2020). Exclusionary zoning prevents non-white people from achieving housing equity (Whittemore 2021). Moreover, many of the realities of urban life in the US that appear to us as "natural" are also the products of a design process. "NIMBY" policies concentrate polluting industries in impoverished neighborhoods, while policies favoring landlords and hamstringing inspections ensure that lead paint continues to be an apocalyptic problem in cities like Baltimore. These are not the unfortunate consequences of neglect nor are they the failures of oversight. These are the products of deliberate design; the city works exactly as it was intended: in opposition to communities.

Yet design has at least one thing in common with PAR methodologies: an emphasis on the future. In some of the initial theorizations of design, Herbert Simon stressed a "broad definition of design as innovation and future-making" (Bargna and Santanera 2020: 27). Similarly PAR is concerned in the end with a desired, future state. Conceived in this way, the two projects of design and anthropology can be construed as complementary, and, as Gunn, Otto and Smith (2013: 3) note, "Although anthropology has an interest in social change and people's imaginations of the future, as a discipline it lacks tools and practices to actively engage and collaborate in people's formation of their future." Design, here, provides the futural orientation. Of course, the difference is that so much of design is a top-down process reflecting the desired futures of corporations and elites, while PAR involves a struggle to achieve a more horizontal approach. However, beginning in the 1970s in Scandinavian countries, and spreading eventually to the United States, a "participatory design" approach began to take shape. In the US, it would coalesce around "user-centered design" in the IT industry (Bargna and Santanera 2020: 27). The ideals, if not the reality, would be similar to the ethos of PAR: design should include people who will be impacted by it.

In reality, and similar, really, to development in general, "user-centered" design practices can merely co-opt people into acquiescing to a top-down design process, now made more palatable with a veneer of "participatory" buy-in, where "co-design processes are subject to co-option by neoliberal forces and that participants risk being coerced and given a false sense of agency while legitimising the political agendas of elites" (Blomkamp 2018: 739). This has certainly been the case with urban design, which typically begins with the collusion of developers and government. In "participatory design theater," people crowd around workshop tables and articulate their hopes and fears on whiteboards and on post-it notes, but the inclusion of communities is largely performative; all of the decisions have already been made. Out of the pluralism of voices, only one has been heard in the end: the ends of capital in the "city as growth machine" (Logan and Molotch 1987).

But does it need to be this way? Krivý and Kaminer (2013: 3) sound a more hopeful note in their critique of urban design as it is often practiced:

> The co-opting of participatory processes by planning departments, the systematic disregard of inequalities, and the empowering of the market resulting from "anti-statism" call for a rigorous evaluation of the participatory turn. Does it necessarily leave inequalities intact? Is it a means of achieving "quietism" by placating the lower middle classes?

The implication here is that, if the needs of people can be articulated and communicated, and if these voices are allowed to impact the design process, then perhaps there is hope for participatory approaches. The method is, ultimately, the most important factor. Even if all parties are acting in good faith, the traditional technologies of design – the focus group, the survey, the workshop, the public hearing – are hardly enough to countenance bottom-up design. And, perhaps, just the opposite: by forcing people into the institutions and discourse of design and development, would-be participatory designers are all but ensuring the reproduction of their own worldviews.

This has been where the development of a design anthropology has been particularly important. Starting with the work of Lucy Suchman in the 1980s, anthropologists began utilizing ethnographic tools in design as a way of articulating insights from collaborative work – a process of translation from user needs and experiences to actual product development (Suchman 1996). And, indeed, much of design anthropology still involves HCI and user-experience (UX) research. The method, though, has been applied to architecture, to urban planning and to a variety of institutions, including psychiatric care and social services (Pink et al. 2020; Campagnaro et al. 2021). What they all have in common is the collaborative and interdisciplinary focus of design techniques. Even if you're doing collaborative work with people who are experts in their lives and in their community, it is unlikely that these same people will have the expertise to, for example, design an app. And that means that your team will most likely include people in programming, and perhaps program management. In other words, design anthropology generally includes a team drawn from both within and without the community, including those without backgrounds in anthropology and participatory research. Although this strident interdisciplinarity makes design research particularly compelling, it also leads to more ethical questions.

Do other experts share the goals of the anthropologist and community (assuming that they are consonant)? There can be differences that seem trivial but have profound implications. For example, we worked on a project where we needed to bring in more GIS expertise. But those researchers were working on billable hours – every phone call, every communication, was charged. Well, yes, time is money, but this had the ironic effect of distancing these collaborators from our project. We simply couldn't afford to have them as full partners, yet using them only for "technical expertise" meant remanding decisions about the project to people without full, collaborative involvement. There's a similar dynamic to other forms of transactional collaboration. Does the illustrator you've engaged to produce your graphic novel share in community aesthetics? Does the crew you've engaged to make your ethnographic film understand the community in which they're working? Do they share in your ethnographic understanding? Design both opens up new possibilities through interdisciplinarity, but it also raises real questions that will have to be addressed; it shares this, as we have discussed above, with multimodality in general.

Design also brings with it a particular temporality. As Bargna and Santanera suggest, "Design has especially stimulated the repositioning of anthropology in relation to time, moving the focus from space to time, and from past to future" (Bargna and Santanera 2020: 29). Typically, design is a goal-oriented process, one that results in future interventions – new websites, apps, re-designed community centers, new "connect-to-care" processes. In applied anthropology, this is nothing new – applied anthropology has an inherent futural orientation. On the other hand, the futures imagined in design are in some ways inimical to anthropology: instrumental, "deliverable" oriented, short-term "fixes" for community problems. In a design project, teams of researchers may conduct interviews, participant observation, and focus groups over an attenuated period of days or weeks before introducing their prototyped "solution." The world of design is a world where problems are (putatively) solved to order.

> A classic example is water filters, which seem constantly to be invented by energetic young designers after a life-changing visit to rural Africa. Take the case of LifeStraw. The LifeStraw solution, like so much design, imagines that a product is enough to address a problem that arises from massive failures of the nation-state and its infrastructure, urban-rural inequalities, social isolation, and so on.
>
> (Chin 2016)

New sleeping bags for the unhoused, bullet-proof backpacks for traumatized US students, micro-credit schemes for women in developing countries. The real problems remain unaddressed, and the "deliverables" not only mark the end of the design research, but actually close off alternatives through an ultimately false resolution. These are examples of "speculative realism," as Peter Redfield has called them, where "the dream of another world remains consciously deferred, caught between inherited expectations, perceived material limits and an attenuated horizon of political possibility" (Redfield 2022: 17). Or, rather, we could simply see this as a plan for forcing others into our own utopia – incrementally improving the lives of others in order to help maintain global inequalities and hyper-consumerism in the West.

On the other hand, what has developed into "design anthropology" is less concerned with product than process. As Ingold writes:

> And in the emerging field of "design anthropology," it is to think of design as an aspect of a process of life whose primary characteristic is not that it is heading to a predetermined target but that it carries on. An anthropology by means of design is precisely this: about how anthropology, through experimental design practice, can help pave the way for sustainable futures.
>
> (Ingold 2016: 7)

In Ingold's version of design anthropology, it is the work of design itself that is the most important outcome of design anthropology, one that brings anthropologists in "correspondence" with practice and making.

Like other instances of design, though, design anthropology is focused on futures – but futures with distinctly different temporalities. For example, designing a new haptic interface for a device is certainly future-focused, but what kind of future are we talking about? One that imagines a world very much like the world we live in now, to be certain, albeit with the improvements brought on by the new interface. While acknowledging that these design processes can also be collaborative, we want to suggest that they also project a flat, impoverished future – not a future at all, to be honest. The future here is exactly the same as the present, a succession of new products that stretches to the horizon without cessation or difference.

A recent volume, *Design Anthropological Futures*, develops Ingold's insight into a subset of design anthropology (Smith et al. 2016). Disavowing both linear and monolithic, end-of-history futures, the contributors to the collection emphasize the future as emergent and multiple, as discourse and practice where the design anthropologist articulates critique, collaboration, and, ultimately, the practice of alternative worlds. That said, if we imagine futures through design anthropology, then we can only do so as a collaborative team that combines transdisciplinary expertise with a highly participatory ethos. Contributors to *Design Anthropological Futures* exemplify that productive tension: drawn from anthropology, art, media, and multiple fields of design, the collaborative future sketched there envisions a creative tension between scholars, activists, and visionaries sharing (sometimes uneasily) a common lexicon of alternative futures. In other words, *Design Anthropological Futures* evokes an anthropology as much informed by multiplicity as intervening within it.

From this perspective, design anthropology is bound up with evocations of "otherwise." As Meek and Morales Fontanilla (2022: 2) explain, "the otherwise conjures latent possibilities and potentialities withheld within a situation or formation; possibilities we might only glimpse obliquely, which are 'prefigured but not formed,' yet that 'hold and open' an otherwise as liberatory transformation." Since it unfolds over a longer period of active collaboration, design anthropology extends the hope that submerged, obfuscated potentialities might be evoked and explored. Not the "new," but the actualization of latencies that were already present in the lived experiences of people. This is what Ernst Bloch called the "not yet," the potentialities for an otherwise that proliferate in our everyday lives, but are never acknowledged in a system that works to actively suppress alternatives and to confine our future to a repetition of the present.

Ultimately, it is this orientation that lifts design anthropology from simply legitimating the status quo through the design of new products or interfaces. Like the "meantime" Redfield describes in his essay on "shacktopia," a multimodal anthropology informed by design anthropology "has, in effect, two horizons: the immediate one, with its prospect of potential reiteration of the present, and a more distant one defined by long-term, potentially utopian desire" (Redfield 2022: 29). Caught between both of these futures, a multimodal approach should acknowledge the shortcomings of the one en route to evocations of the other. The burden of design is precisely this: fighting the inertia of a designed world where the future has been overdetermined as endless iterations of the capitalist present. Every multimodal project needs to confront the question of what constitutes real alternatives, and what can simply be co-opted into the novelty machine of a repetitive capitalism, the "false new" that gives capitalism the appearance of innovation despite its endless repetition of commodity forms (Lefebvre 1991).

Above all else, what helps multimodal anthropology avoid mis-recognizing repetitions of the same as an alternative is the emphasis on collaboration itself, not just in terms of working "together," but in surrendering the power to delegate what kind of "differences" will be acceptable. In contrast, a hackathon may bring together people in the community in order to design new apps with all sorts of potential benefits to community members. But the hackathon itself is structured and channeled in order to subsume real critique into new products, and the "organic intellectual" into an "entrepreneur." As Irani writes:

> In this way, entrepreneurial citizenship subsumes the creativity of the social body while socializing failure. It subsumes hope. It subsumes critique, mutual aid, and desires for better, more just worlds.
> (Irani 2019: 213)

Design 133

In order to ameliorate these tendencies, our multimodal design is structured by PAR methods and includes an iterative, reflective process that acknowledges the tendencies of design to co-opt and appropriate alternative ideas.

Accordingly, we've developed a several step process:

1. Spend time in a community. Although much work in social design takes place over an attenuated timeline, anthropology has generally spent more time in communities than our counterparts in design. Rapport building is a never-ending activity, and it can only be accomplished through the painstaking work of getting to know a place, and building reciprocal relationships with people.
2. Show up with resources. If we define (as we do above) multimodal anthropology as, first and foremost, a collaborative anthropology, then that collaboration is the first order of business. While many things can bring people together, the creation of something new requires new resources. So don't show up with empty hands!
3. Find out what people are doing and have already done. One of the chief lessons of networked anthropology (aka anthropology in a networked world) is that people are consummate experts of their worlds, and that they utilize numerous platforms for their para-ethnographic documentation of their social lives. What videos, Facebook posts, exhibits have been produced (Collins and Durington 2014)? What events celebrate this community, and how do people remember them? Who are the people engaging in this para-ethnographic work? And how can they be integrated as central to the anthropological work?
4. Find out what people would like to do. In some cases, you may be invited to work with people on a specific project, but it is more likely that the needs a community has espoused – while real and urgent – may not be entirely articulated. Also, there's also the question of fit. The anthropologist and their team may be able to help with some things, but others may be beyond their expertise and resources. The first step, in any case, is to build a clear sense of what people in the community want. There are many techniques for this, including needs assessment and asset mapping.
5. Discuss how you can be part of that effort. In multimodal inquiry, the anthropologist's role is delegated by the community itself. That is, multimodality emerges from the needs of the group in consultation with the anthropologist. Rather than showing up with particular media in mind, anthropologists and collaborators consider various media as they develop in the scope of participatory work. What media might be necessary to help realize the goals the community has articulated?
6. Work with groups to model those solutions. Multimodal inquiry presupposes a group of people working together at different capacities: a collaborative inquiry that builds on diverse data in diverse ways. There are various forms of prototyping that anthropologists can utilize.

Prototyping sessions are oftentimes the starting point for participatory inquiry, but we want to stress the five steps that have preceded them, since models that are ultimately produced should be the results of a longer process.

7 Refine and discuss these ideas with stakeholders. Beginning a project inevitably changes a project, and decisions can commit participants to a certain path at the cost of alternatives. This is the "path dependency" that plagues much of the urban US, where hyperbolic investments in automobile infrastructure have led to not only continued investments, but to the foreclosure of alternatives grounded in more safe and sustainable development (Ahangari et al. 2017). It is, therefore, exceptionally important to reconvene early on with initial ideas and prototypes in order to gain consent and incorporate feedback.

8 Implement interventions. One of the promises of design is simply that it *does* something: a proposal for a new park, an exhibit, a new youth program. Design anthropology holds out the promise that anthropology will result in a measurable difference. This can include processes, institutional change, reports, as well as instances of multimodal work – providing they all contribute to the goals of the community.

9 Get feedback from community members. There is no true collaboration unless it includes feedback. Ideally, this should include people beyond the scope of the initial design collaboration, including audiences that the community hoped to influence. What are they understanding from the intervention? And what would make it even more effective?

10 Make changes according to community feedback. Similarly, feedback is pointless if it doesn't lead to change. Once you have feedback, the next stage is to plan changes based on that feedback and, finally, implement those changes.

11 Get feedback – make changes. In addition, this needs to be an iterative process. "Iterative" does not mean, however, "perpetual," yet anthropologists (and designers) have a noticeable habit of disappearing from communities once their research is published. As we've suggested in the chapters above, anthropologists cannot do multimodal work without time, and this attentiveness toward the long duration of fieldwork also needs to extend into the future, if for no other reason than representations themselves can take on a life of their own in a digital age (Collins and Durington 2014).

As we discuss in Chapter 2, following this process is no more a guarantee of a more equitable anthropology than any other element of multimodality. The difference is that – with a design process like this – there are more opportunities for problems and inequalities to be brought to light. In the space of design, uncomfortable questions can be asked.

Using Design Methods in the Field

There are many models for participatory design, including Creative Commons resource guides that take researchers and collaborators step-by-step through an open process. "Research for Organizing" offers one that takes communities through a collaborative process toward social justice goals, while "A Toolkit for Participatory Action Research" focuses on equitable development in Africa. And there are others for all sorts of community development and interventions. Whatever the particular perspective, however, toolkits are generally made up of a variety of worksheets and activities for facilitating participatory processes – methods for engaging community participants and working with them on research (interviews, focus groups) and then analyzing that research in order to plan meaningful change (Hall et al. n.d.). And while toolkits are about prompting community reflection, they also help investigators to avoid some of the pitfalls of hierarchy in community research by using a variety of exercises and techniques to build a horizontal collaboration. A multimodal design anthropology proceeds in much the same way, but with more attention to the media that have enabled the participatory research. While the whiteboards that record the insights of participants in a workshop may be cleaned for the next session, a multimodal anthropology might build those insights into a graphic, a recording, an illustration, and, finally, wireframing and prototypes.

Wireframes

Wireframing is a powerful, collaborative tool: "the basic blueprint that illustrates the core form and function found on a single screen of your web page or application" (Hamm 2014: 15). As a tool, "wireframing" generally represents a step in IT or UX design, and whether it exists on a whiteboard or on an application that simulates the "flow" of the application or webpage, wireframes allow communities to participate together in design without the coding or technical expertise that would otherwise be an obstacle to full participation. Here, it joins other rapid prototyping tools like 3D printing that are associated with product development. In multimodal anthropology, these same tools can help mediate hierarchy and encourage participation. Paper wireframes, for example, allow participants to contribute to the design of IT applications in a very tactile, concrete form that could allow participants to impact design without having any prior technical or design knowledge (Duarte et al. 2018). We have used a variety of wireframes for web and app design, but we also have found it useful to wireframe institutions, processes, and even public spaces. Wireframes are less about the product of collaboration then they are a tangible record of a collaborative process, one that can serve as a touchstone for future discussions. When people wireframe a process like navigating Baltimore's District Court in order to hold landlords accountable for maintaining their properties, multiple insights can be generated regarding bureaucratic obstacles and racism, certainly, as well as ways those power imbalances might be challenged

136 *Design*

or even reversed. While real, institutional change deriving from the wireframe would be an optimal outcome, the wireframes themselves represent powerful artifacts that serve as a critical, ethnographic record of discussions and can even chart the path of future activism as with groups like Baltimore Renters United.

One of our first wireframing projects was in designing community apps with groups of participants in our "Anthropology by the Wire" project. There, we tasked our student researchers with working with community partners in order to wireframe community-focused apps using a wireframing app called POP (Prototyping on Paper), that creates a mock-up of the app using photos of drawings linked together in order to simulate the affordances and flows of the app prototypes. In this exercise, it was the wireframes themselves that were the data, and we analyzed them not only for the different affordances they provided, but for the ways our student researchers envisioned linking them together (Durington et al. 2015). The models showed us the ways media and experience connected together – at least according to our student researchers, and the disconnections there were at least as important as the connections. What did the apps make it easy to do? What was it more difficult to accomplish?

It's also worth extending the idea of wireframes to other applications that may not technically fit that definition. There are urban planning applications that allow one to overlay an AR design on an environment in order, for example, to envision a park or a walkway. Several activists, for example, have been using DALL-E, an OpenAI project that uses prompts to generate digital images. By carefully structuring textual prompts, artists like Zach Katz and Nicole Aptekar have generated hundreds of images of streets transformed into parks and pedestrian paths (Rose 2022). These are not "wireframes" in terms of conventional design, but they can be prompts for discussion and planning. At the very least, they help to articulate a longing for livable cities without the crush of automobiles that has undermined so much of urban life in the United States.

Wireframing Our Suffrage Correspondence Map

A few years later, we worked on another multimodal project that we describe in more detail above in the chapter on mapping. In that project, the first stage was to wireframe the ways we envisioned the map. This had several purposes. First, this wireframe allowed us to enumerate the different affordances we wanted in the software itself. Ultimately, we would consult directly with esri (the company that makes ArcGIS) in order to tweak the template we ultimately used to layer a social network on top of the map. Secondly, the wireframe served as a token in our discussions with a community that included National Park Service staff, historians and student researchers, all of whom participated in what would be the ultimate design and what would make up the data fields for suffrage activists.

In Figure 7.1, we see Susan B. Anthony's connections to other suffrage activists and other places as an epistolary network. This wasn't complete – or

Design 137

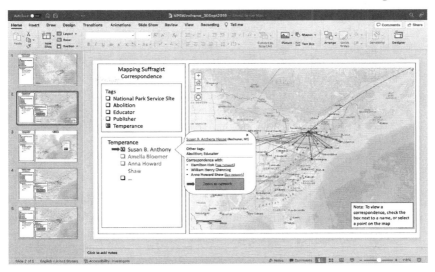

Figure 7.1 Prototyping suffrage

even particularly accurate – but the wireframe served as a proof of concept that allowed us all to design what the platform would look like and how it would enable the discovery of connections between suffrage activists and others (politicians, journalists, spiritualists, etc.).

Prototyping

One of the most powerful tools for a multimodal, design anthropology is the prototype, "an emerging sociomaterial design for our contemporary whose main quality is its permanent 'beta' condition; that is, whose social and material components retrofit each other as being in mutual suspension" (Corsin Jimenez 2014: 343). This is what the design process produces: a prototype, and all of the media that surround it. We can think of the prototype as the materialization of a design anthropology process itself; it is also a launching pad for anthropological inquiry. As Ingold writes:

> We are already used to the idea that the results of anthropological inquiry need not be confined to written texts. They may also include photographs and films. But could they also include drawings, paintings or sculpture? Or works of craft? Or musical composition? Or even buildings?
>
> (Ingold 2013: 8)

If we open up multimodality to include not only forms of representation, but *things*, then we can see the prototype as not just the result of design work, but as a method and as an intervention in the world. Prototype design comes into its own as not just a way of *doing anthropology*, but *doing with anthropology*.

Yet the prototype is hardly the same as "works of craft" or "buildings." Prototypes have a more perfunctory quality, as something that exists in the world, but in a way that implies future negotiation.

> The prototype never quite reaches closure (it is always less than itself, less than one), yet it keeps forking and enabling novel extensions of itself (it is always more than its own self-scaling, it is more than many forms of itself).
>
> (Corsin Jimenez 2014: 348)

The prototype here is an open object. It can be manipulated and utilized, but still promises future versions as the result of design negotiation. As an app, a process, a pedagogy, prototypes intervene in the world without closing off additional collaboration. They are, then, both the product of and the catalyst for design. Ultimately, then, the prototype resides in the future, one that represents the hopes of collaborators and the promises of anthropologies to come. This, then, is a transformative design that goes well beyond IT and UX; we can design the city itself.

Right to the City

Although much of design anthropology has followed the design industry as a whole in its concentration on product development and consumption, a multimodal approach nevertheless acknowledges the ubiquity of design. We live in a designed world, and any interventions we might make in that world are themselves the products of a design process. In writing this, we mean more than a neoliberal commodification of the self, where our experiences of ourselves and others, at even a cellular level, are, to some extent, designed and commodified experiences. We also mean that many of the injustices that characterize life in the United States and elsewhere are the result of design.

"Slow violence," for example, describes "a violence that occurs gradually and out of sight, a violence of delayed destruction that is dispersed across time and space, an attritional violence that is typically not viewed as violence at all" (Nixon 2011: 2). Some of its insidious power comes from its long timescape. Rather than a diluvial moment, the disaster of slow violence unfolds over decades. Glacial and seemingly ineluctable, it finally emerges into the public consciousness as both inevitable and "natural." And yet, for all that it is no less a designed disaster, the product of deliberate policies and racism. When, for example, newspapers report on the astronomical rate of asthma in Baltimore's heavily polluted Curtis Bay neighborhood, they generally do so in terms of a "failure" of government and health policy. Of course, there has been a failure here of basic human rights and a failure of responsibility toward people and the environment, but the high incidence of respiratory illness is still a product of deliberate design, one founded in what Noliwe Brooks has called "segrenomics," "the business of profiting specifically from high levels of racial and economic segregation" (Brooks 2018: 2). That is, concentrating industry in low-income neighborhoods means being able to pollute the environment without consequence.

In this context, Baltimore simply "works" as designed. As the product of over 100 years of segregationist policy and deliberate underdevelopment, the problems of the city are, in the end, designed problems: poverty, abandonment, lead poisoning, chronic absenteeism in schools, high incarceration rates. In other words, Baltimore is designed to produce these outcomes, and changing them means, ultimately, taking on the history of deliberate violence, and challenging each through broad, racial equity strategies and investments.

Instead of this broader, reparative strategy, what has ordinarily happened in Baltimore (and other cities, especially in the United States), is a design that constructs a whitewashed history over the racialized city, resulting in familiar postmodern strategies of selective quotation and re-use – here with the goal of building a revanchist city in the shell of the earlier one. As in the example of Camden Yards (above), an anesthetized B&O station anchors spectator tourism:

> Contemporary consumerist nostalgia as we find it built into Camden Yards instead kills both the dead and the living. It does so by writing over the material traces of past conflicts and injustice, creating instead a mythical historical narrative that silences complexity and suffering. It does the latter by perpetuating anti-black violence, both drawing financial and social support from under-served communities and constructing an urban narrative that does not acknowledge, and cannot accommodate, racism and structural injustice as ongoing cultural and material inheritance.
>
> (Imgram 2015: 327)

We can look at places like Camden Yards (or Baltimore's famed paean to consumer capitalism, the Inner Harbor) as primarily about architecture, and they are certainly that. But it's a good deal more than architecture – it's the design of an experience of the city, and the experience of community. And it includes history, certainly, as well as the buildings that were taken down to build the Yards, but also the parking and transportation, the staff that's (seasonally) employed to serve concessions, the cost of the ticket, the way that the city is visible from Camden Yard's different levels, the tax breaks and incentives that were used to build it, the ways Camden Yards and the M&T Bank Stadium (next door) loom over the neighborhoods that surround them, rendering them an incidental obstacle to spectacle. This is about design, a design that was imposed on the people of the city, and imposed upon the city's history.

Baltimore's segregation, its pollution, its lead poisoning, rat problems, water quality, outdated sewage, homicide rate, etc. – all of these can be seen (as they are often) as the *absence* of design, as problems that "organically" burgeoned under conditions of neglect. We are not minimizing the effects of under-capitalization and disinvestment, merely pointing out that these did not just "happen"; they are the result of conscious policies designed to create a certain kind of urban life. Baltimore is not the result of an accident, but has been purposely designed to function the way that it does.

In opposition to the "city as growth machine" ethos that informs this urban design, we approach it from the perspective of a right to the city:

> far more than a right of individual or group access to the resources that the city embodies: it is a right to change and reinvent the city more after our heart's desire. It is, moreover, a collective rather than an individual right, since reinventing the city inevitably depends upon the exercise of collective power over the processes of urbanization.
>
> (Harvey 2013: 4)

With Baltimore's long history of "segregomics", this can only mean addressing the integrated design at the heart of Baltimore's ruin. As Brown (2021: 184) puts it, this means initiating an integrating and authentic vision of racial equity – one that will ultimately challenge every aspect of Baltimore governance and decision-making. "*Equity does not mean equal* when corrective action is the goal. Racial equity means allocating more resources to redlined communities than are allocated to greenlined communities for as long as it takes to create more equal outcome."

It also means implementing a participatory approach to urban design, one that simultaneously takes a reparative approach to the inequities of planning and decision-making that have been at the core of Baltimore's design:

> Without trust, deep listening, planning with, designing with, cultivating wealthy, and centering lived experience, economic development efforts in Black neighborhoods result in repeated uprootings and economic destruction while deepening cultural dispossession.
>
> (Brown 2021: 251)

The shape of this design is no mystery. We are surrounded by people expressing what design should look like in the context of racial equity. In social movements, in do-it-yourself urbanism, and in both formal and quotidian protest, we can see people proffering design alternatives that seek to re-create the city (Iveson 2013). At its core, the "right to the city" is the right to participate in the city's design – not on a surface level, but on a cellular one where the "right to change ourselves by changing the city more after our heart's desire" means a good deal more than consumption (Harvey 2008: 23). It means being able to participate in every level of the design process, with all of the equity that "participate" should imply.

The principles of that right to the city that informs this approach to design are, after Mulder and Kun (2019) "Hacking," "Prototyping," and "Making." Hacking, here, is "an exploratory, creative way of overcoming limitations in the system" (Mulder and Kun 2019: 227). "Making" and "prototyping" imply conditions under which people are able to utilize tools in order to communicate their vision: "as long as they enable the different stakeholders to collaboratively explore alternatives and to articulate their different viewpoints" (Mulder and Kun 2019: 203). But what does this mean in terms of design anthropology? If we come away from this discussion with an understanding of multimodal design as a series of workshops and focus groups, then we have missed the point entirely. "Participation" here can only mean addressing all of the barriers to full participation, including time and resources. Simply holding a workshop with members of a community whose circumstances prevent them from full participation can only be a parody of real participation. In addition, "participation" cannot truly exist without the acknowledgement of the lopsided, violent design strategies that have worked to oppress people in the past. In other words, we cannot do multimodal design without interrogating what "participation" means in the communities where we work. That critique extends into multimodality itself, into the media we strive to create, and in the impacts we intend that media to have. In short, multimodal anthropology must begin and end with a radical, participatory ethos (Hickey and Mohan 2005).

Classroom Exercises

In the classroom:

1 Re-design the university experience. A good introduction to participatory design starts with the experiences of students themselves as they navigate different offices and divisions within the university, from registration and financial aid through graduation. In many cases, students are critical of their experience, and this can be the inspiration for a critical design anthropology that includes autoethnographic components, workshopping, reflection, and wireframing. An assignment we've used involves several steps:
   a   Getting students in groups of 4–5 people.
   b   Having them collaboratively decide on a part of the university to re-design.
   c   Engaging in autoethnographic journaling to investigate their experiences.
   d   Holding workshops where groups decide on their design intervention.

e Analyzing recordings of workshops in order to generate additional themes and to reflect on the design process.
  f Collaboratively wireframe the re-designed experience.
  g Present the work.

2 Hostile design:
  a Divide the class up into teams and give each a "type" of hostile design. This can include not only what people typically mean by hostile design (architecture, public space), but also laws (e.g., signs), policies, policing, etc.
  b Send teams off to find examples of hostile design and document them using the tools from this text (photographs, apps, storymaps, etc.).
  c Debrief with the class and consider ways to make the city less hostile to the people and communities that inhabit it.

References

Ahangari, H., Atkinson-Palombo, C., & Garrick, N.W. (2017). Automobile-dependency as a barrier to vision zero, evidence from the states in the USA. *Accident Analysis & Prevention*, 107, 77–85.

Bargna, I., & Santanera, G. (2020). Anthropology and design. *Anthropologia*, 7(2), 25–44.

Blomkamp, E. (2018). The promise of co-design for public policy. *Austraulia Journal of Public Administration*, 77(4), 729–743.

Brooks, N. (2018). *Cutting school*. NYL New Press.

Brown, L. (2021). *Black butterfly*. Johns Hopkins Press.

Campagnaro, C., Di Prima, N., & Ceraolo, S. (2021). Co-design and the collective creativity processes in care systems and places. *Social Inclusion*, 9(4), 130–142. https://doi.org/10.17645/si.v9i4.4503.

Chin, E. (2016). Collaboration: Deviation. *Fieldsights*, October 10. https://culanth.org/fieldsights/collaboration-deviation.

Collins, S., & Durington, M. (2014). *Networked anthropology: A primer for ethnographers*. DOI: doi:10.4324/9781315760674.

Corsin Jimenez, A. (2014). The right to infrastructure. *Environment and Plannning D*, 32, 342–362.

Duarte, A.M.B., Brendel, N., Degbelo, A., & Kray, C. (2018). Participatory design and participatory research: An HCI case study with young forced migrants. *ACM Transactions on Computer-Human Interaction*, 25(1), 3.

Durington, M., Gerald Collins, S., & 2014 Anthropology by the Wire Collective. (2015). Games without frontiers. In A. Gubrium, K. Harper & M. Ontanez (eds), *Participatory visual and digital research in action*. Left Coast Press, pp. 259–276.

Fabian, J. (2002). *Time and the other: How anthropology makes its object*. Colombia University Press.

Geertz, C. (1974). "From the native's point of view": On the nature of anthropological understanding. *Bulletin of the American Academy of Arts and Sciences*, 28(1), 26–45. https://doi.org/10.2307/3822971.

Gunn, W., Otto, T., & Smith, R.C. (2013). *Design anthropology theory and practice*. Bloomsbury Academic.

Gupta, A., & Stoolman, J. (2022). Decolonizing US anthropology. *American Anthropologist*, 124(4), 778–799.

Hall, R., Brent, Z., Franco, J., Isaacs, M., & Shegro, T. (n.d.). *A toolkit for participatory action research*. Internal Development Research Centre. www.tni.org/files/publication-downloads/a_toolkit_for_participatory_action_research.pdf.

Hamm, M. (2014). *Wireframing essentials*. Packt Publishing.

Harvey, D. (2008). The right to the city. *New Left Review*, 53, 23–40.

Harvey, D. (2013). *Rebel cities: From the right to the city to the urban revolution.* Verso.

Hickey, S., & Mohan, G. (2005). Relocating participation within a radical politics of development. *Development and Change*, 36(2), 237–262.

Imgram, C. (2015). Building between past and future. *Philosophy and Social Criticism*, 41(3), 317–333.

Ingold, T. (2013). *Making*. Routledge.

Ingold, T. (2016). *Lines: A brief history* (1st edn). Routledge. https://doi.org/10.4324/9781315625324.

Ingold, T., & Gatt, C. (2013). From description to correspondence: Anthropology in real time. In W. Gunn, T. Otto, & R. Charlotte-Smith (eds), *Design anthropology: Theory and practice*. Bloomsbury, pp. 139–158. www.bloomsbury.com/uk/design-anthropology-9780857853691/.

Irani, L. (2019). *Chasing innovation*. Princeton University Press.

Iveson, K. (2013). Cities within the city. *International Journal of Urban and Regional Research*, 37(3), 941–956.

Jordan, S. (2003). Who stole my methodology? *Globalisation, Societies and Education*, 1(2), 185–200.

Kindon, S., Pain, R., & Kesby, M. (2009). Participatory action research: Origins, approaches and methods. In S. Kindon, R. Pain, & M. Kesby (eds), *Participatory action research approaches and methods: Connecting people, participation and place*. Routledge, pp. 9–19.

Krivý, M., & Kaminer, T. (2013). Introduction: The participatory turn in urbanism. *Footprint*. DOI: doi:10.7480/footprint.2.766.

Lamphere, L. (2018). The transformation of ethnography. *Human Organization*, 77(1), 64–76.

Lefebvre, H. (1991). *The production of space*. Blackwell.

Liu, R. and Shange, S. (2018). Towards thick solidarity. *Radical History Review*, 131, 189–198.

Logan, J.R., & Molotch, H.L. (1987). *Urban fortunes: The political economy of place*. University of California Press.

Meek, L.A., & Morales Fontanilla, J.A. (2022). Otherwise. *Feminist Anthropology*, 3(2), 274–283.

Mulder, I., & Kun, P. (2019). Hacking, making, and prototyping for social change. In Y.M. de Lange & M. de Waal (eds), *The hackable city*. Springer, pp. 225–239.

Nixon, R. (2011). *Slow violence and the environmentalism of the poor*. Harvard University Press.

Phillips de Lucas, A. (2020). Producing the "highway to nowhere": Social understandings of space in Baltimore, 1944–1974. *Engaging Science, Technology, and Society*, 6, 351. doi:doi:10.17351/ests2020.327.

Pink, S., Duque, M., Sumartojo, S., & Vaughan, L. (2020). Making space for staff breaks. *Health Environments Research and Design Journal*, 13(2), 243–255.

Redfield, P. (2022). Shacktopia. *Social Anthropology / Anthropologie sociale*, 30(2), 16–33.

Rose, J. (2022). Artists are using AI to imagine cities without cars. *Vice*, July 29. www.vice.com/en/article/epzznk/artists-are-using-ai-to-imagine-cities-without-cars.

Rosenberger, R. (2017). *Callous objects*. University of Minnesota Press.

Smith, R.C., Tang Vangkilde, K., Gislev Kjaersgaard, M., Otto, T., Halse, J., & Binder, T. (eds) (2016). *Design anthropological futures* (1st edn). Routledge. https://doi.org/10.4324/9781003085188.

Sousa, J.W. (2022). Liberating community-based research. *Engaged Scholar Journal*, 8(3), 1–12.

Suchman, L. (1996). Reflections on a work-oriented design project. *Human-Computer Interaction*, 11, 237–265.

Whittemore, A. (2021). Exclusionary zoning. *Journal of the American Planning Association*, 87(2), 167–180.

Wolf, E.R. (1982). *Europe and the people without history*. University of California Press.

8 Conclusion

We were associate editors (along with our colleague Harjant Gill) of the multimodal section in the *American Anthropologist* from 2017–2019, just as it changed from being the "visual anthropology" section. The table below shows the media highlighted in different issues during the two volumes of the journal that we worked on.

119(1)	*119(2)*	*119(3)*	*119(4)*	*120(1)*	*120(2)*	*120(3)*	*120(4)*
Film	Film		Film	Film	Film	Film	Film
	Photo						
		Design					
			Drawing		Drawing		
				Zine			
				App			
					Games		
						Open access	
						Multimedia	
							Sensory ethnography
							Virtual tour

We can conclude many things from this simple table. First, film was a constant over our tenure – as it continues today. One of our beliefs (and one borne out in the table) is that multimodal anthropologies has been less about getting people who would have otherwise engaged in visual anthropology than it is about enlisting people who would have otherwise consigned themselves to text-based ethnographic work. In other words, multimodal anthropology is about

DOI: 10.4324/9781003330851-9

presenting anthropologists and the people with whom they work with more options for dissemination and communication.

At first glance, the table seems to imply a direction – toward more multimedia, toward more digitization. We would also reject this idea. Instead, what we've found is that, over time, people have been able to represent different aspects of work they've done and, to the extent that we succeeded as associate editors, it was in making a space for those diverse media. But making that space was not an easy task. Deborah Thomas, then the editor of *American Anthropologist*, had proposed a website that would present material alongside the journal that couldn't go into print (or a pdf). However, our discussions about this site raised many questions. Would content appearing on the site have a stable link? Could that content link to the journal? Was this a published journal? With an ISSN? Or something else? How could we cite material appearing on this site? Technical issues aside, the biggest obstacles were, ultimately, about corporate control. *American Anthropologist* is paywalled, and the publisher was unwilling to link back to the journal from the non-paywalled website. Accordingly, there are no DOI (digital object identifier) links for the web content. It was difficult, therefore, to convince contributors that this was as prestigious or permanent as publishing an article with the journal, even though wonderful material has been published there over the last five years.

This experience negotiating with our publishers is a synecdoche for multimodal anthropology. As we've written throughout this book, multimodal anthropology is not new, and it does not represent a "break" with the past. Just the opposite: the development of multimodal anthropology returns us to the past in a flash of recognition for some unresolved possibility or unacknowledged ancestor. Multimodal anthropology articulates moments in anthropological encounters that have heretofore not often been represented in anthropology. Drawings, for example, have a long history in the field, but with the advent of multimodal anthropology, there have been more and more possibilities for publishing illustrations, graphic novels and other art. Similarly, anthropologists have long played, used, and designed various sorts of games in their research, but the concept of publishing an anthropologically intended game is something that is comparatively new in the field. So why now? The easiest answer is that there are more opportunities in publishing digital content. Of course, these same digitally enabled opportunities also represent limitations: corporate ownership, limited access, digital divides. As we discuss above, multimodality foregrounds certain ethical dilemmas as a condition of its articulation, and each new articulation of multimodality confronts us with the contradictions of capitalism.

And while we're happy to have been multimodal editors at *American Anthropologist*, we acknowledge that there are areas of multimodal scholarship that we were not able to explore in the section. The future will assuredly give rise to different areas of multimodal content, and, along with them, attendant obstacles and ethical concerns. Yet it will only represent a portion of that anthropological work. If we think about the entire scope of multimodal collaboration, the entirety of ethnographic sensorium, then the media that make up published multimodal anthropology are only momentary flashes on a continuum of possibilities. Some of these forms may resist reification into a published form. For example, exhibits, performance, design, games: all of these exceed the limited representations that may appear on websites or in published texts. Missing, for example, are the discourse and practice that accompany them. At the very least, the collaborative elements of our multimodal practice are rarely preserved in more than a highly etiolated form in the products of ethnographic work – an illustrative, discursive exchange, a photo that captures a moment of ethnographic work.

Ephemerality and the Multimodal

In 2019, we went to a Baltimore Museum of Art workshop with several non-profits from the Greenmount West neighborhood. The goal of the workshop was to increase co-operation between these diverse non-profits and to plan a future for their community together. We were there with Ms. Betty Bland-Thomas, the President of the South Baltimore Partnership, in order to show them our Sharp Leadenhall Walking Tour and talk about that as a collaborative process. There were several activities that the workshop facilitators led us through that were all wonderful examples of collaborative design, but one of the most striking was the sketchnoting: a wall of dynamic, graphic representations of our dialogues, rendered expertly by the artists and generating new ideas and connections through the combination of text, illustration, and symbol (Hollands 2018). Unlike, however, Hollands's sketches of the American Anthropological Association Annual Meeting (published in the multimodal section of the *American Anthropologist*), the drawings that accompanied our workshop have disappeared; they were part of a collaborative, multimodal moment that survives only in a few photographs and notes. Like most of the fieldwork that we do, media here proved ephemeral.

It need not always be that way, of course. Arguing for a "sounded anthropology," Samuels et al. (2010: 338) critique the "essentialization" of sound as ephemeral and, therefore, resistant to ethnographic analysis:

> Scholars and composers have long suggested that one of the difficulties posed by sounds, as compared with images, is the inability to extract sounds from their temporal constraints. Sound recording allows for the temporal dislocation of a sound from its time and place of origin, but does not facilitate the ability to do the auditory equivalent of sustaining the gaze on an image for as long or as short as one desires. Thus even though sounds can be reproduced and replayed, sound is often considered to have, by its nature, a kind of temporality that the visual may not share.

148 *Conclusion*

The essay is an eloquent argument for anthropological work on soundscapes, an argument that has borne fruit; the American Anthropological Association's "Music and Sound Interest Group" continues to grow, while soundscape studies have long been a part of the EASA (European Association of Social Anthropologists) conferences and workshops. If anthropologists can represent soundscapes in our work, than other senses – and other experiences – can be represented as well.

Yet for every soundscape that anthropologists study, or exhibits that anthropologists publish as an article or a catalog, there is still a vast reservoir of ephemerality. Even digital materials themselves have proved elusively temporary: "Digital media is not always there. We suffer daily frustrations with digital sources that just disappear. Digital media is degenerative, forgetful, erasable" (Chun 2008: 160). On our "Anthropology by the Wire" website, a Tumblr account that archives our four-year, NSF-sponsored project, you will find diverse media produced by our students – photographs, films, essays, along with links to interesting sites and archival materials. Or you might not. Many of the links on this site are already broken, just seven years after the project's completion. We're not upset by this. Multimodal anthropology is filled with ephemeral moments, and the digital media that we've produced is just as susceptible to contingency and change.

Note in Figure 8.1 the conspicuous absences from our site as links fade away.

Which is why we made the conscious decision to archive media on a YouTube channel for posterity (Figure 8.2).

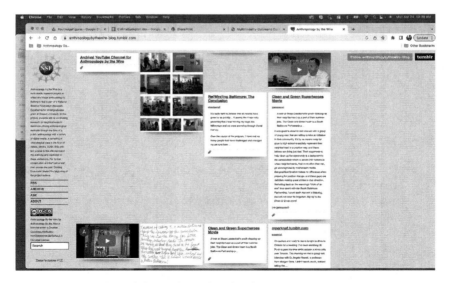

Figure 8.1 Screenshot of the Anthropology by the Wire main site

Conclusion 149

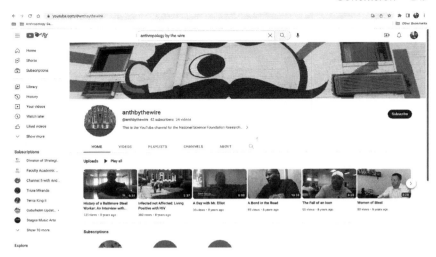

Figure 8.2 Screenshot of Anthropology by the Wire YouTube channel

Imagine Figure 8.3 as the entirety of one's multimodal fieldwork – all of the preparations, all of the people, all of the collaborations. All of the observations, communications, meetings, exhibits, workshops, articles, films, games, apps – everything. The dark lines represent those moments that have been abstracted and reified into some form of media, but there's still a vast surplus out there, some of which (the darker shades) persists in forms that could still coalesce into some form of dissemination. The lighter areas, however, represent more ephemeral encounters and fleeting media connections. These moments may or may not be part of multimodal ethnography – after all, sometimes the ephemeral should remain just that, a moment in a stream of experience. On the other hand, others have tried to document those moments, as has been the case with social media researchers focusing on ephemeral, digital content (Bainatti et al. 2021). The ephemeral, though, brings with it multiple ethical concerns. Just as it would in more conventional ethnography.

Yet in that surplus, we still might find cause for hope and optimism (Willow 2023).

Figure 8.3 Multimodal spectrum

150 *Conclusion*

Multimodal Futures

One way to conclude our discussion of multimodal anthropology might be to prognosticate on its future. What will come next in multimodality? Of course there will be new digital applications, new ways of recording, new platforms for social media and for collaboration. Doubtless, these will be revelatory of new forms of multimodal dissemination. Ultimately, though, writing a final chapter on technologies of "the future" would be to fall into a deterministic trap we've tried to avoid in this book. The "multimodality" we've described here is the multimodality of collaborative anthropology through media, social action, and networked connection. In other words, a continuum of social life and practice. Some of those multimodal moments will become "materialized" in multimodal forms – a film, an article, an app, a game. Many of them will remain ephemeral.

On our "Anthropology by the Wire" Tumblr, some of the materials that remain accessible amidst the wreckage are some photos of an exhibition we co-sponsored at the Hamilton Gallery in Baltimore (Figure 8.4). Joining some of the people in the community who were exhibiting their own photography, we presented what we had done and invited people to share their own thoughts and recollections. Nearly all of that moment is gone, although many of the photographs produced by the community have been published in a book, *Life Don't Have to End* (Barazotto 2013). Could we have published a 360 degree video of the event? Something on YouTube? Could this have become something more Instagrammable?

Figure 8.4 Photo from the Anthropology by the Wire exhibit

We Have Always Been Multimodal

We submit that these are not the questions that we should be asking. Instead, we think of multimodality as a series of eddies in a stream of anthropological work. The duration of anthropological work is (partially) visible through these eddies, Bakhtinian chronotopes that order those experiences according to different temporalities that connect, and reconnect in slightly different ways, becoming productive, in some cases, of their own ethnographic vectors. These "eddies" cannot be reduced to technologies, yet, as we have suggested, digital platforms have helped (but also channeled and constrained) the quality of those localizations. Illustrations may have been part of anthropology since the Torres Straits expeditions, but it is the advent of digital tools that makes the reproduction of images so much more accessible than in pre-digital halftone printing, just as numerous apps have made comic illustration more approachable than the print-only era.

And yet this, too, should not be seen as a technological development. Our media are also embedded in platforms which, themselves, are a source of agency, adding meaning, commodifying, and connecting our work in complex ways to corporations, the state, and to hegemonic structures of racism, neocolonialism, but also, hopefully, to formations of resistance. The platforms that enable artists to upload their content are also sources of deep inequality, exacerbating a system of corporate control (Duffy 2017). Other platforms open up possibilities for more democratized content, as with the growth of Sci-Hub (which, of course, initiates other inequalities) (Maddi and Sapinho 2022).

Multimodal Moods

Even as it evidences many of the same field dilemmas that have always vexed anthropologists, multimodal anthropology is always emergent because the constellation of people, media, and power is continuously shifting. However, more than a "problem" that needs to be "solved," this characteristic of multimodal anthropology is its theoretical impact; multimodal anthropology will continue to demand that we interrogate the grounds of collaboration, the meaning of sharing, and the impact of the work that we do. In our conclusion, we evoke the future of multimodal anthropologies not as applications of some new technology, but as continuing challenges to what it means to do anthropology and to produce ethnography. This, after all, is its lasting contribution: to precipitate reflection on what we could do and what we could become. In order to sketch this future, we take a page from the late anthropologist Robert Textor's ethnographic futures research to evoke an "optimistic," "pessimistic," and "most probable" future for multimodal anthropology (Mead and Textor 2005). In the end, of course, the question of what multimodal anthropology will look like is really a question of the fate of anthropology in general.

Optimistic: We would love to see multimodal anthropology proliferate into undergraduate and graduate programs. Beyond that, we would love to see multimodal methods dissolve some of the boundaries between anthropologists and the communities in which they work. If we embrace a variety of media and platforms as part of our multimodal work, then we should acknowledge that people are quite capable of documenting their lives and theorizing on their significance. In lives suffused with media and media platforms, multimodal anthropology is less a specialized subfield than a general condition of existence. In this optimistic future, the role of anthropologist evolves into a facilitator and amplifier, helping communities know what they already know and assisting them in sharing that knowledge where it needs to be shared – on the forums and platforms that make the most sense.

Realistic: As Ernst Bloch reminds us, we only undermine ourselves if we limit "reality to what has become real" (Bloch 1996: 157). Yet, it seems likely that the growth of multimodal anthropology will be a bumpy ride, one accompanied by considerable ethical reflection. The moment we introduce new platforms, especially digital platforms, a vespiary of issues emerges that demand that we attend to power, politics, and intersectional identity. Ultimately, those ethical moments are constitutive of this multimodal moment. The growth of multimodal inquiry cannot exist apart from a critical examination of the imbrication of multimodal platforms in systems of power. As, for example, Twitter devolves into a platform for fascist apologists and disinformation, so, too, does the meaning of that platform for multimodal anthropology change.

Pessimistic: In their analysis of anthropology hiring and employment, Speakman et al. (2018) find the field to be dominated by a few elite departments – a seeming stranglehold of nepotism and oligarchy. In this pessimistic scenario, any innovation in anthropology is quickly sublimated to the domination of elite faculty in elite programs. Here, changes in the field merely shore up the existing status quo. This is hardly a new development, and similar charges have been leveled against anthropology's "postmodern" and "ontological" turns, each portraying itself as a radical break with the old, even as these same theoretical invocations tended to buttress the very same elite programs. Theoretical paradigms may change, but anthropologists remain merchants of the strange (Kapferer 2013; Todd 2016). Yet although this more pessimistic extrapolation is certainly possible (and, indeed, has happened several times before), it seems to us less likely than the first two. As a collaborative endeavor that spills across multiple media, the establishment of expertise and authority that accompanied the growth of photography and film in visual anthropology, to give two examples, does not seem as assured – and certainly not a linear process. The slow (and uneven) institutionalization of visual anthropology has led to a white, cisgender canon of filmmakers, one that presumes a Western, elite background (Gill 2021). If multimodal anthropology describes a shifting constellation of media, collaboration, and engagement, could such a canon coalesce around people and institutions? Perhaps – but it seems less likely, if only because multimodal anthropology will remain a boundary object of sorts, with different communities of anthropologists and interlocutors all engaged in different practices, different analyses and, ultimately, different instantiations of the multimodal. Nevertheless, the pessimistic projection involves the continuation of digital divides as before – some people will be able to use diverse media to represent communities, and others – however adroit in their media production – will not be granted the authority.

References

Bainatti, L., Caliandro, A., & Gandini, A. (2021). From archive cultures to ephemeral content, and back. *New Media & Society*, 23(12), 3656–3676.

Barazotto, C. (2013). *Life don't have to end*. Firsty Design Publishing.

Bloch, E. (1996). *Principle of hope*. MIT Press.

Chun, W.H.K. (2008). The enduring ephemeral, or the future is a memory. *Critical Inquiry*, 35, 148–171.

Duffy, B.E. (2017). *(Not) getting paid to do what you love: Gender, social media, and aspirational work*. Yale University Press.

Gill, H. (2021). Decolonizing visual anthropology. *American Anthropologist*, 123(1), 36–49.

Hollands, C. (2018). A hand-drawn conference review. *American Anthropologist*, 120(2), 348–352.

Kapferer, B. (2013). How anthropologists think. *Journal of the Royal Anthropological Institute*, 19, 813–836. https://doi.org/10.1111/1467-9655.12066.

Maddi, A., & Sapinho, D. (2022). On the culture of open access: The sci-hub paradox. *Research Square*. DOI:doi:10.21203/rs.3.rs-2357492/v1.

Mead, M., & Textor, R.B. (2005). *The world ahead: An anthropologist anticipates the future*. Berghahn Books.

Samuels, D.W., Meintjes, L., Ochoa, A.M., & Porcello, T. (2010). Soundscapes: Toward a sounded anthropology. *Annual Review of Anthropology*, 39(1), 329–345.

Speakman, R.J., Hadden, C.S., Colvin, M.H., Cramb, J., Jones, K.C., Jones, T.W., et al. (2018). Market share and recent hiring trends in anthropology faculty positions. *PLoS ONE*, 13(9), e0202528. https://doi.org/10.1371/journal.pone.0202528.

Todd, Z. (2016). An indigenous feminist's take on the ontological turn. *Sociology Lens*, 29(1), 4–22.

Willow, A.J. (ed.). (2023). *Anthropological optimism: Engaging the power of what could go right* (1st edn). Routledge. https://doi.org/10.4324/b23231.

Postscript
The Elephant in the Room

"We are in a different experiential world – one not necessarily inferior to reading a text, but to be understood differently."

(MacDougall 2006: 270)

Readers at this point may be wondering where does ethnographic documentary film reside in multimodal anthropology and why have we discussed it sparingly in this book? Well, the elephant in the room is that we decided not to talk about ethnographic film except to discuss some of the parameters for the practice, dissemination, and reception of ethnographic film as a precedent for a multimodal anthropology. Discussions of ethnographic film provide us with some grounding questions we ask about multimodal anthropology. We saw it fitting as a postscript rather than guiding the conversation, as it usually does in visual anthropology. As we have articulated in multiple instances, we do not see multimodal anthropology replacing visual anthropology and, therefore, ethnographic film. Ethnographic film is often seen as synonymous with visual anthropology. That has created tensions for the inclusion of audio, photography, experimentation, and other media and practices. It continues to plague many of the experiments in filmmaking such as virtual reality that anthropologists and their collaborators are playing with. Yet, we would be remiss to not provide a reader that is new to multimodal anthropology with some context for ethnographic film.

Simply moving ethnographic film productions and self-contained linear films into the parameters of what is considered multimodal anthropology would give both short shrift. Rather, ethnographic film can be a practice within multimodal anthropology but neither should be limited by the other. Just as we critique the move to a so-called digital anthropology to supplant fieldwork during the COVID pandemic, simply relabeling ethnographic film as multimodal anthropology is intellectually lazy. Some of the hand wringing over what is ethnographic film, who can produce it, and how should it be received has been the prominent trope in visual anthropology for years and does provide some of the tensions that inform a multimodal anthropology today. Many ethnographic filmmakers have already shown disdain for multimodal anthropology and that's fine. Perhaps it is because it reduces

DOI: 10.4324/9781003330851-10

the authority of the auteur? Maybe it is because a multimodal anthropology is centered on collaboration... real collaboration. Or, maybe it is being perceived as a threat to supplant visual anthropology. As Jay Ruby told Durington shortly before his death after reading our invitation to multimodal anthropology in 2017, "So, you essentially want to kill ethnographic film and visual anthropology." Not so much.

Although the meaning and form of ethnographic film has been questioned since its inception, it is often synonymously linked with visual anthropology as its defining practice. And, therefore, perhaps no other term in the lexicon of visual anthropology is more insular and contested than ethnographic film. This is especially true as a number of non-linear new digital media forms and modes of internet distribution are becoming prevalent in the 21st century that have opened up collaborative possibilities and multimodal practice. These technological developments, like many that have come before it such as sync-sound recording and the advent of videotape, occur alongside the contestation of what the project of ethnography actually entails and by what methods it is practiced in the larger field of anthropology. The question has been, and remains, is film or video a legitimate methodological tool in anthropological fieldwork, and, if so, does it possess the capacity to convey or contain ethnographic knowledge? The same challenges face multimodal anthropology methods.

As the topic and practice of visual anthropology has increased in popularity both within and outside of the discipline of anthropology, there is a continuing need to discuss the parameters of what actually constitutes the ethnographic film, its defining medium. If the reader is looking for resources for this there are fine bibliography entries for both visual anthropology, ethnographic film, and the more nuanced notion of ethnographic documentary production. When contemplating the inclusion or evaluation of media in the genre one is often faced with the dilemma of what criteria define ethnographic film and filmmakers. Often, the question is whether or not any determinate criteria or boundaries should exist at all. The same challenge faces a burgeoning conceptualization of multimodal anthropology, and many of the postulations over ethnographic film, its canon, and practice inform those discussions now.

The history of ethnographic film in the 20th century is well documented with a recognized corpus of films and filmmakers consistently cited as the intentional or unintentional harbingers of the practice. As evidenced by countless syllabi for ethnographic film and visual anthropology courses, many see the production of Robert Flaherty's *Nanook of the North* as the first example of what could be considered an ethnographic film. This is primarily due to Flaherty's focus on an exotic non-Western culture, long considered the main focus of anthropology, and the stated intent throughout the film to depict the "real life" of the Inuit. Although Flaherty was not an anthropologist and, therefore, did not adhere to ethnographic methodology in his practice, he is often celebrated for the fact that he spent so much time with the Inuit and attempted to reflect an indigenous perspective, if not a personal relationship, in the construction of the narrative of the film by working with his main "informant" (Nanook) throughout the filmmaking process. The fact that there was no anthropological intent, identity, or methodology in *Nanook of the North* places Flaherty and the film comfortably within the genre of ethnographic film as a standard. After all, who needs anthropology to produce an ethnographic film? As we asked earlier, did Flaherty consider Nanook a collaborator? If so, that opens up an interpretation of this corpus of work as a form of multimodal anthropology. But we do know this was not the case so there is no need to reclaim it as such. Yet, there have been attempts at participatory ethnographic filmmaking as discussed in the book that influence and guide multimodal anthropology.

As the discipline of anthropology continued to develop in the 20th century the medium of film was looked upon as a means of not only presenting culture, but as a possible objective methodological tool in the recording of data about culture during the fieldwork process, much like photography. Thus, the notion of utilizing film as a means of obtaining objective research footage cross-culturally was celebrated and advocated by Margaret Mead and others. In the early manifestations of the filmmaking process in anthropology a debate has ensued up to the present day surrounding the use of film in anthropological methodology. Should the camera be used simply as a supposedly objective data collection device to produce footage for other anthropologists to analyze, or should the ethnographic filmmaker also be concerned with constructing a cohesive narrative and structure with a concern with aesthetics to make films palpable for a wider audience? It is a debate that reflects the struggles between positivist and subjective positions in the field at large. (MacDougall 2006) It also overemphasizes the capacity of filmmaking to capture "reality." As Brian Winston has aptly observed, maybe "this objective-subjective stuff is a lot of bullshit" (Winston 1995: 159). The idea that film could capture objective "data" to create comparable research footage would ground ethnographic film well into the 1960s and beyond serving as the rationale for the establishment of both the Film Study Center at the Peabody Museum and the Smithsonian Human Film Archives. Beginning with Mead and Bateson's fieldwork approach in Bali which resulted in "Trance and Dance in Bali" and the archetypical "Bathing Babies in Three Cultures," the methodological practices of using long shots and aiming for whole bodies in the filmmaking process would mark the yearning for objectivity.

The decades of the 1960s and 1970s witnessed a critical evaluation of the anthropological project as the field was simultaneously "reinvented" (Hymes 1972) to become more inclusive of marginalized groups and practices in order to be "re-evaluated" (Clifford and Marcus 1986) in the postmodern era and "recaptured" (Fox 1991) in the 1990s. Simultaneously, this era was an active time in the development of ethnographic film as strong institutional funding and changes in film technology in the 1960s and 1970s supported a flurry of activity. Many ethnographic films produced at this time are considered classics and continue to be part of any analysis of film in visual anthropology. In the 1980s and 1990s films began to focus on individuals or themes without a necessary concentration on providing comparative or objective data. While many still advocated an approach to filmmaking, classification, and utilization that emulated staid anthropological practice, others were quite revolutionary in their approach.

One of the most stifling notions of the varied discussions of ethnographic film has been the need to taxonomically define what it is and what it is not. The need to break away from this approach provides the same questions that undergird a multimodal anthropology. As Reddy states:

> it seems that prescriptive formulations of what ethnographic films are should give way to an acceptance of a variety of techniques that serve the diversity and specificity of the subjects themselves and which are better suited to the particular relationship that exists between the filmmaker and participant.
>
> (Reddy 2015)

It is the latter sentiment that has marked the most productive ethnographic film engagements, principally in the personal ethno-fictions of Jean Rouch who we see as a spiritual guidepost for multimodal anthropology. The important point here is that when collaboration is the primary focus of an ethnographic film, it tends to produce the most meaning for an audience. So, what is an ethnographic film? What is multimodal anthropology? These tensions over defining both signal an exciting intellectual field and a set of ambiguities that leave many uncomfortable. Just as MacDougall sees ethnographic film for its potential to create a "different way of knowing" (MacDougall 2006), we see multimodal anthropology as a means to explore new epistemologies and collaborative possibilities.

This dilemma over what constitutes an ethnographic film can be a bewildering experience. Oftentimes when one is introduced to ethnographic film they are also introduced to cultural anthropology. It's a lot to take in simultaneously; 1) the field of anthropology and its multi-varied focus on the concept of culture, 2) the set of methods that constitute ethnography as a practice, and 3) the medium of film that has an expansive representative and generative capacity as a way of creating meaning. As Jay Ruby noted, there is no "standard agreed-upon definition of the genre" of ethnographic film except that in popular parlance ethnographic film tends to be thought of as any documentary about "exotic" others (Ruby 1996: 1345). While this may seem problematic, it is in fact quite reflective of anthropology writ large. The fact that there is no centralized notion of what actually entails ethnographic film places it in the same position as the central concept of anthropology itself since no agreed-upon definition of culture exists in the field at large either.

The dilemma has persisted in consideration of ethnographic film. As MacDougall has pointed out "the nascent field of visual anthropology was at that time conceived almost exclusively in terms of ethnographic film" (MacDougall 2006: 264). Yet, when challenged to define ethnographic film, most elide the question entirely by declaring which films are not ethnographic (Loizos 1993). Or, one begins to catalog an exhaustive set of criteria that supposedly determine an ethnographic film (Heider 2006). The most famous source for these criteria is the book *Ethnographic Film* by Karl Heider, which often serves as the gateway for those pursuing an interest in ethnographic film and visual anthropology in general. The criteria outlined exhaustively by Heider in 1976 tend to revolve universally around the subject of the film, the intention of producers, shooting and presentation style, and the identity of the creator just to name a few in a very close reflection of the original methods proposed by Mead and Bateson. Ethnographic film discussions have not benefited from these proscriptive recommendations and neither will multimodal anthropology.

Heider goes about the task of forming a set of "attributes of ethnographic film" to determine the "ethnographicness" of particular films in the genre. According to Heider, "these are attributes that are common to all films, however ethnographic they may be. Most of these attributes are really continua. And films can be located somewhere along the line of variation" (Heider 2006: 50). Thus, Heider proposes a shopping list of attributes to be utilized in the analysis of any film claiming to be ethnographic with the results being placed on a continuum with one end being "ethnographic" and the other being something else entirely. One has to appreciate the efforts of Heider to replace the limited notions of dichotomous thinking with the efforts to provide a more malleable, and hence inclusive and realistic, notion of what ethnographic film might entail through its classification on a continuum of practice and form. Some of the attributes on this continuum include both technical and theoretical notions that range from the "appropriateness of sound" to the inclusion of a sense of "wholeness" regarding bodies, interaction, and people (Heider 2006). In this sense, Heider's criteria for defining and evaluating ethnographic film are reflective of the desire to root the practice in some form of objectivity. Heider provides an "attribute dimension grid" for individuals to use in their evaluation of the classic ethnographic films that he engaged, and films that might be possible future inclusions in the genre. Yet, even in the second edition of perhaps the most famous book in ethnographic film studies in 2006, Heider still laments a reality that has yet to come into play, "Ideally, ethnographic films unite the art and skills of the filmmaker with the trained intellect and insights of the ethnographer" (Heider 2006: ix). Again, we can derive some influence from ethnographic film discussions around "wholeness" in particular, but we would be limited to start to develop an "attribute dimension grid" for multimodal anthropology followed by claim-making exercises for what is and isn't.

The uniting thread throughout the entire body of literature on ethnographic film is a questioning of what connotatively defines the "ethnographic" in ethnographic film and the utilization of a corpus of work for analysis and discussion that still defines the field today; the collected work of a handful of filmmakers "that are best known and most widely available" (Heider 2006: xiii). Through the evaluation of the established canon of ethnographic films principally made up of works by John Marshall, Timothy Asch, Robert Gardner, Jean Rouch, and David MacDougall, a host of authors have attempted to define ethnographic film form and practice. These discussions tend to move between a hope that whatever entails ethnographic film practice and makes up ethnographic film stays firmly entrenched in anthropology; while others attempt to move the genre further away from what are considered the constraints of the field. Grounded in a larger notion of anthropology as the "study of human action as sociocultural performance," Ruby has suggested "ethnographic film should be grounded in the assumption that culture is created, maintained, and modified through social acts of communication" (Ruby 2000: 242). At the other end of the spectrum, Bill Nichols has advocated that whatever defines ethnographic film in the end should be developed by those outside of anthropology all together. Sound familiar? We see these notions informing efforts of collaboration and communication in a multimodal anthropology.

Perhaps the most easily understood definitions of ethnographic film rely on content as the primary criterion for evaluation. The audience engages tropes usually associated with anthropology writ large including an exotic subject, in an equally exotic locale. Conceptions of ethnographic film that rely on form are reflective of various shooting strategies and forms of presentation that have developed over time. In this sense, the way in which a film is conceived, shot, and edited conforms to, or combines, a variety of filmmaking production methods that in the end resemble something "ethnographic" in presentation of form. The choice of which form to pursue often dictates the ethical parameters that one is working under as well. As MacDougall cautions, is the filmmaker a "self-effacing machine" or does one engage the cultural contact situation and move into more participatory modes of filmmaking practice? Or perhaps the ethnographic is found through experimental and even fiction-based forms as seen in the work of Jean Rouch? Is multimodal anthropology seen in the collaborative possibilities and experimentation with different forms of mediums and epistemologies? Very similar questions are they not?

Although potentially damned in perpetuity by the limited interpretive and aberrant readings frighteningly described and still prescient today by Martinez (1992), ethnographic film and the overall visual anthropology project continues to retain some hope in realizing the overall humanistic anthropological project that encourages cultural relativism by simply revealing another way of life. In perhaps the most radical approach to ethnographic film and visual anthropology uttered since the conception of the field,

MacDougall, invoking Deleuze, calls for "New Principles of Visual Anthropology" that engage the "prelinguistic aspect of film" in order to engage the emotive and sensory aspects of our, and others', social lives (MacDougall 2006: 269). Perhaps contradictory to this but engaging contemporary media forms, others claim that the future of visual anthropology is to be found in multilinear and multimodal forms to communicate ethnography (Graizborg and McPike 2020).

So, is ethnographic film dead? That is the question. If one considers the medium of celluloid film itself and the technical parameters that came with it, yes. And we should engage a different term that is not so conceptually loaded. But the hegemony of the term "ethnographic film" will not fade in time as it is now treated synonymously with the entire practice of ethnographic media production regardless of the medium. Essentially, to discuss ethnographic "film" now is to conduct a historical survey of a form that is no longer functional for contemporary anthropology. Perhaps the most beneficial practice would be to place ethnographic film in an archival position and discuss the potential of ethnographic media that engages new modes of production and dissemination and seeks to engage the criteria that one would use to define ethnographic film historically and today. In this sense, we agree with the critical evaluative project of Pink to "re-situate visual anthropology's practices and rethink its identity in terms of its relationship with other areas of anthropological theory and methodology" (Pink 2006: 131). It is this latter intent that brings into question the capacity of ethnographic film to keep pace with "anthropological theory and methodology" as these trajectories begin to move beyond standardization and lineal containment.

In an era where the very future of anthropology as a relevant discipline is being questioned, visual anthropology and ethnographic film in particular are mediums through which the unique contributions of an anthropological perspective can be made palpable to a wider audience that would benefit from a culturally relativistic worldview and a paramount concern for the socioeconomic and political positions of local populations throughout the world. Yet, just as we are inclined to rethink visual anthropology, we must also rethink the concept of ethnographic film, the standard bearer of visual anthropology for the uninitiated and the form of visual anthropology most closely associated with the sub-discipline. Inevitably, the idea of creating a set of criteria for defining what is included in a genre is a limiting and unproductive exercise. As many films are left out of the discussion or brought into an antagonistic relationship with it, the genre model is quickly exhausted.

Yet, ethnographic film continues to flourish as a genre. One only needs to peruse the films that have been part of the Society for Visual Anthropology Film and Media Festival and the Royal Anthropological Institute Film Festival to see the amount of media being produced. It is an exciting time for visual anthropology and ethnographic film and we encourage the reader to explore both of those topics thoroughly. After all, if one hasn't borne witness to Napoleon Chagnon in a black speedo then you are missing out.

References

Clifford, J., & Marcus, G. (1986). *Writing culture: The poetics and politics of ethnography*. University of California Press.

Fox, R.G. (1991). *Recapturing anthropology: Working in the present*. School for Advanced Research.

Graizbord, D., & McPike, J. (2020). Features and form: Appropriating digital storytelling for public ethnography. Ethnography.

Heider, K.G. (2006). *Ethnographic film* (revised ed.). University of Texas Press. https://doi.org/10.7560/714588.

Hymes, D.H. (1972). *Reinventing anthropology* (1st edn). Pantheon Books.

Loizos, P. (1993). *Innovation in ethnographic film: From innocence to self-consciousness, 1955–1985*. University of Chicago Press.

MacDougall, D. (2006). *The corporeal image: Film, ethnography, and the senses* (student ed.). Princeton University Press. www.jstor.org/stable/j.ctt4cgb17.

Martinez, W. (1992). Who constructs anthropological knowledge? Toward a theory of ethnographic film spectatorship. In P. I. Crawford & D. Turton (eds), Film as ethnography.Granada Centre for Visual Anthropology.

Pink, S. (2006). *The future of visual anthropology: Engaging the senses*. Routledge.

Reddy, P. (2015). The emergence of ethnographic film practice: Past travels and future itineraries. www.africanfilmny.org/2011/the-emergence-of-ethnographic-film-practice-past-travels-and-future-itineraries/.

Ruby, J. (1996). Visual anthropology. In D. Levinson & M. Ember (eds), *Encyclopedia of cultural anthropology*. Henry Holt and Company, Vol. 4, pp. 1345–1351.

Ruby, J. (2000). *Picturing culture: Explorations of film and anthropology*. University of Chicago Press.

Winston, B. (1995). *Claiming the real: The documentary film revisited*. British Film Institute.

Index

Abolitionist anthropology 39
Actor Network Theory (ANT) 111
Affordances 1, 12, 15, 111–117, 136
African GoPros 26
Anishinaabeg 100
Anthropological revanchism 81, 128, 139
AnthropologyCon 6, 101, 105–106
Anthropology of Visual Communication 18, 20–24
ArcGIS 83, 85–86, 136
Asset mapping 78, 86, 105
Astacio, Patricia 11, 13, 31, 43
Augmented Reality (AR) 118–119
Autoethnography 101

Bad habitus 11, 31
Baltimore: Camden Yards 81, 139; Curtis Bay 88–89, 138; dollar homes 87; Free Your Voice 88; Greenmount West 50, 86–87, 89, 150; Inner Harbor 87, 139; lead paint 38, 128; media 50–51, 69, 73; Movement Against Destruction (MAD) 87; Poppleton 82–83; redlining 79, 90; Sharp Leadenhall 32–33, 81, 87–88, 147; University of Maryland Medical Center (UMMC) 82
Baltimore Museum of Art (BMA) 86, 147
Bateson, Gregory 8, 17, 23, 58, 94, 156, 158
Becker, Howard 66
Benjamin, Walter 20
Black butterfly 48, 79
Blogging 15, 72,
Boas, Franz 43, 45, 61–63
Brown, Lawrence 48, 79

Camden Yards (Baltimore) 81, 139
CAMRA 24

Candyland (Game) 98
Cards Against Anthropology (Game) 96
Chin, Elizabeth 8, 26–29
Collaborative anthropology 2–7, 12–13, 16, 29–30, 38, 46, 113, 117, 125, 133, 150
Comcast 48
Correspondence 15–18, 84–85, 131
COVID 1, 25, 30, 48–49, 63, 154
Creative commons 51–52, 98, 100, 135
Creative misuse 117–118
Crowdsourcing 86
Culture area 80
Curtis Bay (Baltimore) 88–89, 138
Curtis, Edward 63, 65

Daily round 10, 101–102, 105
Dattatreyan, Gabriel 13, 15, 31
Decolonization 2, 39, 126
Democracy and Dictators (Game) 94
Digital divide 2, 5, 14, 30, 38, 43–44, 47–52, 112, 146, 153
Digital Matatus 80
Dogon people 44, 80
Dollar homes (Baltimore) 87
Douglass, Frederick 87

Echo chambers 12, 50
Enclosure 78
Ephemerality 147–150
EthnoAlly 113–114
Ethnographic Terminalia 8, 20, 27, 31, 72
Extractivism 46, 80

Facebook 14, 15, 29, 49, 112, 117, 133
Favero, Paolo 26, 31, 71–72, 113–114
Feld, Steven 19
Free Your Voice (Baltimore) 88

Galton, Francis 60–61
Game mechanics 96–97, 99–101
Gameworld 95
Gentrification 32, 46, 50–51, 81, 86–89
Glass, Aaron 65–66
Google Street View 101–103
Greenmount West (Baltimore) 50, 86–87, 89, 150
Gross, Larry 22–23, 57
Growth machine 6, 81–83, 129, 140
Guardian of the Snacks 25–26
Gupta, Akhil 2, 126
Gupta, Hemangini 12–13, 25

Hackathon 132
Hall, Vera 41
Haptics 100
Harper, Krista 68–69
Heider, Karl 159–159
Hostile design 88, 128, 142
Human subjects 38–41
Hunt, George 45, 65

Inner Harbor (Baltimore) 87, 139
Instagram 10, 28–29, 42, 150
Intellectual property 52
IRB (Institutional Review Board) 38–40
Itch.io (website) 96, 98, 105
Ivins, William 66
izi.TRAVEL (website and app) 32, 86–89

Knight Lab 86. 90, 117, 119

Laboratory of Speculative Ethnography 26
Lacks, Henrietta 39
Long Day of Young Peng, The (Game) 97, 100
Loy Loy (Game) 96

MacDougall, David 156–160
Malinowski, Bronislaw 16, 21, 30
Map My Run (App) 117
Mead, Margaret 8, 17, 23, 45, 58–59, 94, 105, 156, 158
Minecraft (Game) 99, 106
Mizer, Nick 94, 100, 101, 104, 106, 107
Movement Against Destruction (MAD) 87
Multimedia 3, 7, 12–13, 15, 32, 46, 68, 78, 83, 88, 112–113, 125–126, 145–146
Multimodality and Society 25

Nanook of the North 155–156, 57–58
National Park Service (NPS) 85, 86

NSF (National Science Foundation) 39, 148
Not-Yet 90

Open access 49, 98, 145
Otherwise 43, 90, 132, 135

Participatory Action Research (PAR) 5, 56, 68, 125, 135
Path dependencies 112, 134
Photovoice 66, 68–70
Photo Elicitation 67–70, 73–74
Pitt Rivers Museum 8, 17, 93
Poppleton (Baltimore) 82–83
Powis, Dick 15, 28–29
Prototyping 72, 101, 105, 113, 116, 130, 133–138, 141

Qualitative Data Analysis (QDA) software 110

Residential security maps 79
Right to the city 138, 140–141
Riis, Jacob 61–62
Role Playing Game (RPG) 94, 96
Rouch, Jean 21, 23, 31, 41, 45, 57, 68, 157, 159
Ruby, Jay 23, 58, 67, 70–71, 155, 157, 159
Ruins 51

Sketchnoting 147
Segregation 139–140
Segrenomics 139
Sensory ethnography 24, 26, 95, 145, 160
Shankar, Arjun 13, 31, 69–70
Sharp Leadenhall (Baltimore) 32–33, 81, 87–88, 147
Slow violence 38, 138
Speculative realism 131
Stoller, Paul 21, 27, 93
Storymapping 82, 85, 90
Studies in Visual Communication 23, 66
Suffrage 136–137, 84–86

Temple X 88
Thick description 97, 101
Thing From the Future, The (Game) 96
Thomas, Deborah 10, 24, 25, 146
Thousand Year Old Vampire (Game) 101
Torres Strait 7, 17, 151
Traditional Knowledge (TK) license 52
Twine 97–98, 119–123
Tylor, Edward Burnett 17
Tyranny of structurelessness 50

University of Maryland Medical Center (UMMC) 82
User Experience (UX) 110, 114, 129, 135, 138
Utopia 90, 131

WhatsApp 14, 15, 48, 117
Wide Angle Youth Media 33, 74, 88
Wireframing 113–114, 116

Worth, Sol 22–23, 57

X (formerly Twitter) 29, 111, 112, 152

YouTube 10, 15, 50, 110, 148–150

ZOME 118–119
Zoom 1, 127

9781032362243